AF131133

The Language of Taxonomy

The Language of Taxonomy

AN APPLICATION OF SYMBOLIC LOGIC
TO THE STUDY OF
CLASSIFICATORY SYSTEMS

By JOHN R. GREGG

ASSOCIATE PROFESSOR OF ZOOLOGY, COLUMBIA UNIVERSITY

NEW YORK 1954
COLUMBIA UNIVERSITY PRESS

COLUMBIA BICENTENNIAL EDITIONS AND STUDIES

The Energetics of Development
BY LESTER G. BARTH AND LUCENA J. BARTH

New Letters of Berlioz, 1830–1868
TEXT WITH TRANSLATION, EDITED BY JACQUES BARZUN

*On the Determination of Molecular Weights by
Sedimentation and Diffusion*
BY CHARLES O. BECKMANN AND OTHERS

LUIGI PIRANDELLO: *Right You Are*
TRANSLATED AND EDITED BY ERIC BENTLEY

The Sculpture of the Hellenistic Age
BY MARGARETE BIEBER

The Algebraic Theory of Spinors
BY CLAUDE C. CHEVALLEY

HENRY CARTER ADAMS
The Relation of the State to Industrial Action
AND *Economics and Jurisprudence*
EDITED BY JOSEPH DORFMAN

ERNST CASSIRER
The Question of Jean-Jacques Rousseau
TRANSLATED AND EDITED BY PETER GAY

The Language of Taxonomy
BY JOHN R. GREGG

Ancilla to Classical Reading
BY MOSES HADAS

JAMES JOYCE: *Chamber Music*
EDITED BY WILLIAM Y. TINDALL

Apokrimata: Decisions of Septimius Severus on Legal Matters
EDITED BY WILLIAM L. WESTERMANN AND A. ARTHUR SCHILLER

Library of Congress Catalog Card Number: 54-9363

COPYRIGHT, 1954, COLUMBIA UNIVERSITY PRESS, NEW YORK
PUBLISHED IN GREAT BRITAIN, CANADA, INDIA, AND PAKISTAN
BY GEOFFREY CUMBERLEGE, OXFORD UNIVERSITY PRESS
LONDON, TORONTO, BOMBAY, AND KARACHI
MANUFACTURED IN THE UNITED STATES OF AMERICA

General Editor's Preface

The modern university has become a great engine of public service. Its faculty of Science is expected to work for our health, comfort, and defense. Its faculty of Arts is supposed to delight us with plays and exhibits and to provide us with critical opinions, if not to lead in community singing. And its faculty of Political Science is called on to advise government and laity on the pressing problems of the hour. It is unquestionably right that the twentieth-century university should play this practical role.

But this conspicuous discharge of social duties has the effect of obscuring from the public—and sometimes from itself—the university's primary task, the fundamental work upon which all the other services depend. That primary task, that fundamental work, is Scholarship. In the laboratory this is called pure science; in the study and the classroom, it is research and teaching. For teaching no less than research demands original thought, and addressing students is equally a form of publication. Whatever the form or the medium, the university's power to serve the public presupposes the continuity of scholarship; and this in turn implies its encouragement. By its policy, a university may favor or hinder the birth of new truth. This is the whole meaning of the age-old struggle for academic freedom, not to mention the age-old myth of academic retreat from the noisy world.

Since these conditions of freedom constitute the main theme of Columbia University's Bicentennial celebration, and since the university has long been engaged in enterprises of public moment, it was doubly fitting that recognition be given to the activity that enlarges the world's "access to knowledge." Accordingly, the Trustees of the University and the Directors of its Press decided to signalize the 200th year of Columbia's existence by publishing some samples of its current scholarship. A full representation was impossible: limitations of time and space exercised an arbitrary choice. Yet the Bicentennial Editions and Studies, of which the titles are listed on a neighboring page, disclose the variety of products that come into being on the campus of a large university within a chosen year. From papyrology to the determination of molecular weights, and from the state's industrial relations to the study of an artist's or poet's work in its progress toward perfection, scholarship exemplifies the meaning of free activity, and seeks no other justification than the value of its fruits.

JACQUES BARZUN

Foreword

Taxonomy proper and *methodological taxonomy* are closely related departments of taxonomic inquiry, yet they differ in several interesting ways.

In the first place, their *subject-matters* are different. At basis, taxonomy proper is concerned with the realm of living or extinct organisms. Taxonomists who are engaged in the pursuit of taxonomy proper observe, describe, and classify animals and plants and formulate and test general laws or theories of certain kinds that are suggested by their classificatory systems. Methodological taxonomy, on the other hand, does not deal with organisms at all—not directly, that is—for it is a branch of taxonomy whose concern is with the resolution of philosophical issues generated by the results of taxonomical research, or with nomenclatural rules, or with the critical assessment of alternative hypotheses set forth in taxonomy proper, or even with the writing of introductory textbooks expounding the aims, methods, and results of taxonomic biology. In brief, the primary domain of inquiry for taxonomy proper is the organic world, whereas the domain of methodological taxonomy is taxonomy proper itself.

These two taxonomical activities are distinct in another and still more obvious way: their *vocabularies* are different. Their vocabularies are different simply because their subject matters are different, and terms that are indispensable in the language of the one may not even have a significant use in the language of the other. For example, 'hermaphroditic' is a term in taxonomy proper that is correctly applicable to some organisms, but as a methodological term it has no apparent use. Conversely, 'latinized binomial' is a methodological term that is true of most species names, but it has no discoverable application to animals or to plants. Clearly, taxonomy proper and methodological taxonomy are carried on in different languages.

Taxonomy proper and its methodological counterpart differ in a third way: as sciences, they are *unequally developed*. Taxonomy proper is an ancient biological science—as old, perhaps, as biology itself—and it has gradually come to possess a technical vocabulary of considerable descriptive subtlety and power. To see how advanced its language is, one need try only the simple experiment of describing the inflorescences of various plants, first with, and then without, the help of such words as 'spicate,' 'umbellate,' 'racemose,' 'capitate,' 'corymbose,' and other terms commonly used in taxonomic botany. Methodological taxonomy, on the other hand, is a relatively primitive science. Aside from a sparse technical vocabulary especially created for use in nomenclatural studies, it has practically no linguistic apparatus comparable in usefulness and precision to that doing service in taxonomy proper. Taxonomists engaged in methodological research are thus without adequate linguistic resources to support their investigations. They must rely almost entirely upon unsuitable prescientific idioms borrowed from everyday language. As a result, methodological taxonomy languishes while taxonomy proper pushes rapidly ahead.

The purposes of this book are two.

First, it has been written to suggest that the symbolic methods of modern formal logic are useful and appropriate tools for the prosecution of methodological research in the foundations of taxonomy. In particular, it is designed to draw the attention of biologists to a discipline called *set-theory*, which lies on the borderline between elementary logic and elementary mathematics. Set-theory provides a systematization of some highly general ideas centering around the notion of set, class, aggregate, manifold, or collection that seem made to order for use in the methodological treatment of taxonomic classificatory systems. Accordingly, the first three sections of the book are devoted to expounding the elements of set-theory in a semiformal manner that may interest taxonomists and biologists in general.

Second, it is intended to illustrate the methodological utility of set-theoretical methods by using them to reconstruct the neo-Linnaean concept of taxonomic classificatory system. The design and construction of classificatory systems is taxonomy proper *sine qua non*, yet, owing to the lack of suitable methodological terminology, the available descriptions of such systems are nearly all deficient in clarity and rigor. The last three sections of the book are offered as a first step to improve this situation. Biologists may find the treatment of classificatory systems contained therein intriguing for its novelty alone, but a careful perusal of it may yield some new insight even to seasoned taxonomists.

Whatever its merits, this book owes much to my friend Richard Lewontin, who has done his best to instruct me in the rudiments of modern taxonomy, and for whose advice I am most grateful. I also wish to thank the Rockefeller Foundation for a fellowship during the tenure of which a large part of the work of writing this book was done.

John R. Gregg

Contents

Contents

The Language of Taxonomy

1. Sets

A basic concept of set-theory is that of membership in a set. To say that y is a set and that x is a member of it we shall adopt the simple notation:

(1.1) $(x \in y)$

In this expression, the Greek letter epsilon is taken as shorthand for the phrase 'is a member of (the set),' so that '$(x \in y)$' can be given the reading 'x is a member of (the set) y'. This little set-theoretical formula, with its variables 'x' and 'y', can be used in the construction of actual statements by replacing 'x' and 'y' by suitable designative expressions. What is meant here by 'suitable,' however, will take a little explaining. Let us suppose that it were possible to classify all designative expressions (e.g., 'Charles Darwin,' 'the present Queen of England,' 'the Harvey Society,' 'the set of all taxonomic groups,' 'the set of all taxonomic categories,') into those designating concrete, spatiotemporal objects (we shall say that any such object is an *individual*), those designating sets of individuals, those designating sets of sets of individuals, those designating sets of sets of sets of individuals, and so on. We might then agree to call the first group of expressions, those designating individuals, N^1; the second group of expressions, N^2; the third group, N^3; the fourth group, N^4; and so on. Clearly, 'Charles Darwin' would belong in group N^1, 'the Harvey Society' in group N^2; and, as we shall later see, 'the set of all taxonomic groups' will belong to N^3, and 'the set of all taxonomic categories' to N^4. Now, expressions from any of these groups are suitable for replacing

'x' and 'y' in '$(x \in y)$,' *with the proviso* that if the one replacing 'x' is chosen from group N^i, then the one replacing 'y' must be chosen from group N^{i+1}. No replacements that fail to satisfy this proviso will result in the formation of a statement. (These brief remarks have to do with the interpretation of set-theoretical formulae. Actually, some restrictions have to be placed upon the construction of the formulae themselves in order to prevent the occurrence of certain set-theoretical paradoxes. The formulae in this essay are constructed in such a way as to satisfy a body of restrictions called the *theory of types*. A lucid account of this theory, and of alternatives to it, is to be found in Quine [1950], especially pp. 225–252.)

Let us now try to produce some actual statements by interpreting (1.1) in this manner. If we let 'NAT' designate the set of nineteenth-century naturalists, then '(Charles Darwin $\in$ NAT)' will state that Charles Darwin is a member of this set. Similarly, if we let 'D' designate the Democratic Party, then '(Harry Truman $\in$ D)' asserts the membership of Harry Truman in this set of individuals. Furthermore, if we let 'P' designate the set of all political parties, then '(D $\in$ P)' makes the claim that the Democratic Party is a member of this set. Thus, 'Harry Truman' is a name in group N^1, 'D' is a name in group N^2, and 'P' is a name in group N^3. It follows from the proviso on choosing names to flank '$\in$,' that '(Harry Truman $\in$ P)' is not a statement at all: a conclusion that common sense supports, for it is clear that if the names of all political parties were listed, the name 'Harry Truman' would not appear on the list.

One final point, before we turn to other set-theoretical notations. It should be apparent that a choice of suitable expressions to replace 'x' and 'y' in '$(x \in y)$' may result in the formation of a *false* statement. For instance, if we let 'C' designate the set of twentieth-century chemists, then '(Charles Darwin $\in$ C)' is a statement, but it is false.

Given a set x and a set y, we shall say that x *is included in y,* or briefly, ($x \subset y$), just in case every member of x is also a member of y. This usage of the expression 'is included in' can be fixed by the following rule:

(1.2)   ($x \subset y$) if and only if, for all z, if ($z \in x$) then ($z \in y$).

To take some very prosaic examples: if 'O' designates the set of all owls and 'C' designates the set of all carnivores, then (O $\subset$ C), for every owl is a carnivore; and if 'A' designates the set of all anthropoids and 'M' designates the set of all mammals, then (A $\subset$ M), for every anthropoid is a mammal. It will follow from this usage of 'is included in' that every set is included in itself:

(1.3)   For all x, ($x \subset x$),

for this is just to say that every member of x is a member of x. A further consequence is that if x is included in y and y is included in z, then x is included in z:

(1.4)   For all x, y, and z, if ($x \subset y$) and ($y \subset z$) then ($x \subset z$).

From the statement that the set of men is included in the set of mammals and the further statement that the set of mammals is included in the set of animals, we are entitled by (1.4) to conclude that the set of men is included in the set of animals.

Another useful set-theoretical concept is that of set identity. To say that a set x is identical with a set y, or, briefly ($x = y$), will be regarded as equivalent to saying that x is included in y and also that y is included in x, and this, in view of (1.2) is just to say that any member of either set is also a member of the other. The rule following will serve to fix this convention for easy reference:

(1.5)   ($x = y$) if and only if ($x \subset y$) and also ($y \subset x$).

Some trivial examples of set-identity statements are: '(the set of molluscs = the set of molluscs)' and '(the set of taxonomists

= the set of biosystematists).' Less picayune uses for the notion of set-identity will be found in the sequel.

It should be noted that (1.5) is applicable only to sets. We are thus left with no means of expressing identity of individuals. But this deficiency can be removed by adopting '$(x = y)$' as a meaningful but undefined expression when x and y are both individuals. Thus, when it proves useful, we can employ the identity sign '$=$' in such contexts as '(Charles Darwin = the author of *The Origin of Species*)'; but such cases cannot, of course, be translated into statements about set-inclusion.

A further point that should be mentioned in passing is this: although two wholly different expressions may flank the identity sign in an identity statement, yet, when such a statement is true it is about—at most—one thing, namely, the joint designation of those two expressions.

The decision to construe set-identity as mutual inclusion is a most far-reaching one, some of whose consequences for understanding the structure of taxonomic systems will be described in later pages. In the meantime, we shall point out two purely formal consequences. (These hold for individuals as well as for sets.) The first of these is that every set is identical with itself:

(1.6)   For all x, $(x = x)$.

The second is that when a set x is identical with a set y and y is identical with a set z, then x and z are identical:

(1.7)   For all x, y, and z, if $(x = y)$ and $(y = z)$ then $(x = z)$.

Both of these results should be obvious enough after a little reflection.

Identity statements must often be *denied* as well as *asserted*. To deny that x is y we shall put a stroke through '$=$' in '$(x = y)$':

(1.8) $(x \neq y)$ if and only if it is *not* the case that $(x = y)$.

This convention is self-explanatory, and will not require exemplification at this point.

Having come into possession of the identity sign let us put it at once to good use. It is frequently advantageous to be able to construct a designation for a given set by enumerating its members. In fact, this is an excellent method of defining sets that are otherwise difficult to identify. Let us use '$\{x\}$,' for example, to designate the set whose sole member is x, '$\{x,y\}$' to designate the set whose sole members are x and y, and, in general, '$\{x_1, x_2, \ldots, x_n\}$' to designate the set whose sole members are $x_1, x_2, \ldots, x_n$. These curly-bracket notations are easily introduced in terms of identity:

(1.9) ($\{x\}$ = the set in which any z is a member if and only if $(z = x)$).

(1.10) ($\{x,y\}$ = the set in which any z is a member if and only if $(z = x)$ or $(z = y)$).

(1.11) ($\{x_1, x_2, \ldots, x_n\}$ = the set in which any z is a member if and only if $(z = x_1)$ or $(z = x_2)$ or $\ldots (z = x_n)$).

Some wholly obvious examples are these: $\{$Gargantua$\}$ is the set whose sole member is the late famous gorilla Gargantua; and $\{Homo\ sapiens,$ Animalia$\}$ is the set whose sole members are the taxonomic groups *Homo sapiens* and Animalia. Hence, it is trivial that (Gargantua ϵ $\{$Gargantua$\}$), and that (*Homo sapiens* ϵ $\{Homo\ sapiens,$ Animalia$\}$).

We come now to some set-theoretical concepts that are, perhaps, a shade less familiar than the foregoing. The *complement* $\bar{x}$ of a set x is the set of all nonmembers of x:

(1.12) ($\bar{x}$ = the set in which any y is a member if and only if it is *not* the case that $(y \ \epsilon \ x)$).

If, for example, A is the set of all alligators, then its complement $\bar{A}$ is the set of all non-alligators. Thus we will have as true the statement that (Gargantua ϵ $\bar{A}$), for it is *not* the case that

(Gargantua ϵ A). Gargantua, furthermore, is a member of the complement of the set of men, of the set of conifers, and of the set of bacteria—to mention some obvious examples.

The *overlap* $(x \cap y)$ of a set x and a set y is the set of all members common to x and y:

(1.13) $((x \cap y)$ = the set in which any z is a member if and only if $(z \epsilon x)$ and also $(z \epsilon y))$.

Suppose, for illustration, that R is the set of all members of the Republican Party, and V is the set of all people from Vermont. Then $(R \cap V)$ is the set of all Republicans from Vermont. Calvin Coolidge, e.g., is a member of $(R \cap V)$. Again, let B be the set of all birds, and let A be the set of all Antarctic organisms. Then $(B \cap A)$ is the set of all Antarctic birds. Sum- and complement-notations can be combined in interesting ways. Thus $(R \cap \overline{V})$ is the set of Republicans who are not from Vermont, and $(\overline{R} \cap V)$ is the set of Vermonters who are *not* Republicans. Members of the latter set are scarce. Similarly $(\overline{B} \cap A)$ is the set of Antarctic organisms other than birds and $(B \cap \overline{A})$ is the set of all birds save Antarctic ones.

The *sum* $(x \cup y)$ of a set x and a set y is the set in which any thing is a member just in case it is a member of x or else of y or of both x and y, i.e., of *at least one* of x and y:

(1.14) $((x \cup y)$ = the set in which any z is a member if and only if $(z \epsilon x)$ or $(z \epsilon y))$.

For examples of set-sums we do not have far to turn. Let F be the set of all fresh-water fish and M be the set of all marine fish. Then $(F \cup M)$ is the set of all fresh-water fish together with all marine fish. Indeed, if we let 'FS' designate the set of all fish, we shall have the true identity-statement '(FS = $(F \cup M))$.' Some highly artificial set-sums can be found. One is the sum $(L \cup O)$ of the set L of all locomotives and the set O of all orchids. Each locomotive is a member of this set and so is each orchid. Such cases are mentioned because they are sometimes useful, as we shall later see (page 46).

Two sets of very special methodological utility are *the universal set* UN and *the empty set* EM. The universal set may be specified as the set to which anything belongs that satisfies some condition that is satisfied by everything. We have already come across a condition of this sort, for, as we have seen (1.6), everything is self-identical. Thus, the use of 'UN' can be fixed by citing the following rule:

(1.15)   (UN = the set in which any x is a member if and only if $(x = x)$).

Thus UN is the set to which *everything* belongs. EM, on the other hand is the set to which *nothing* belongs. It is most readily defined as the complement of UN: for, if everything is a member of UN then, clearly, nothing can be a member of its complement:

(1.16)   (EM = $\overline{\text{UN}}$).

To say that a given set is devoid of members is merely to say that it is identical with EM: thus, if J is the set of Brazilian jaguars, then '(J = EM)' is the false claim that there are *no* Brazilian jaguars; and if R is the set of Arctic rhinoceri, then '(R = EM)' is the true claim that it has no members. Contrariwise, to say that a given set *has* members is merely to deny that it is empty: hence '(J $\neq$ EM)' is the true claim that there are Brazilian jaguars and '(R $\neq$ EM)' the false claim that there are Antarctic rhinoceri.

An especially important use of 'EM' permits one to assert that two sets are mutually exclusive (have no members in common) by asserting that their overlap is empty. Thus, if Y is the set of all yew trees and W is the set of all walnut trees then to say that ((Y $\cap$ W) = EM) is to say that nothing is both a yew tree and a walnut tree. Similarly, if P is the set of all political parties and S is the set of all scientific fraternities, then '$((P \cap S) = EM)$' asserts that no political party is a scientific fraternity, and vice versa. Again, '$(((\{Gargantua, Toto\} \cap \{Toto, Bushman\}) = EM)$' is the assertion that the mentioned set overlap is empty—but this statement, of course, is false, for this overlap is just $\{Toto\}$, the set whose sole member is Toto, and $(\{Toto\} \neq EM)$.

The sign 'UN' will figure prominently in future developments, and at those times its use will be explained. We shall forego discussion of its methodological utility for the time being, therefore, and shift our attention to a somewhat new topic: namely, sets whose members are *ordered pairs*.

2. Sets of Ordered Pairs, or Relations

The ordered pair whose first constituent is x and whose second constituent is y will be designated by:

(2.1) $(x;y)$.

If x and y are not identical, then the expression:

$(y;x)$

will designate an ordered pair distinct from $(x;y)$, i.e., it will designate the ordered pair whose first constituent is y and whose second constituent is x. Let us call each of two such pairs the *reverse* of the other.

Now the notions that were developed in the preceding section for sets in general are to be regarded as applying to sets of ordered pairs in particular; so the next step in developing a notation for discourse about sets of ordered pairs will consist in carrying over the use of 'ϵ' to express set-membership. Thus, the expression:

(2.2) $((x;y) \; \epsilon \; z)$

can be read as asserting that the ordered pair $(x;y)$ is a member of the set z of ordered pairs. Alternatively, it can be read as asserting that x bears the relation z to y, for it is fruitful to regard sets of ordered pairs as relations between the constituents of ordered pairs. We shall sometimes choose the one reading and sometimes the other. But more often we shall combine them in a hybrid idiom '$(x;y)$ is a member of the relation z,' for this construction is at once convenient and suggestive of the continuity of the present section with §1.

The other notations of the preceding section are reconstrued in analogous fashion. The complement $\bar{z}$ of a set z of ordered pairs is the set of all ordered pairs that do not belong to z. The overlap ($w \cap z$) of a relation w and a relation z is the set of all ordered pairs that belong both to w and to z. The sum ($w \cup z$) of a relation w and a relation z is the set of all ordered pairs that belong either to w or to z. The curly-bracket notation can be used as before: $\{(x;y)\}$, for instance, is the relation whose sole member is $(x;y)$, and $\{(x;y), (y;x)\}$ is the relation whose sole members are $(x;y)$ and $(y;x)$. Furthermore, a relation w is included in a relation z just when every ordered pair belonging to w also belongs to z, a relation w and a relation z are identical just in case they are mutually inclusive, a relation z is identical with the empty relation EM just when there are no ordered pairs in z, and a relation z is identical with the universal relation UN just in case every ordered pair is a member of z.

Some actual examples may help to make these points clearer. Consider, for instance, the set of ordered pairs in which any pair $(x;y)$ is a member just in case x is father of y. Let us designate this set, or relation, by 'MP.' Then, clearly, we shall have '((Erasmus Darwin;Charles Darwin) ϵ MP),' for Erasmus Darwin is father of Charles Darwin; and we shall also have '((George VI;Elizabeth II) ϵ MP),' for George VI is father of Elizabeth II. But neither of the pairs (Charles Darwin;Erasmus Darwin) and (Elizabeth II;George VI) is a member of MP, for Charles Darwin is not father of Erasmus Darwin, and Elizabeth II is not father of George VI. Under suitable membership conditions, however, a pair and its reverse may both be members of the same set of ordered pairs. For example, if we let 'CS' designate the relation in which any pair $(x;y)$ is a member just in case x is cousin of y, then if we have '($(x;y)$ ϵ CS)' we shall also have '($(y;x)$ ϵ CS),' for if x is cousin of y then y is cousin of x. Similar remarks are true also of the relation FCS in which any ordered pair $(x;y)$ is a member just in case x is first cousin of y, for y will also be first cousin of x. By way of further example, we may note that $((\text{MP} \cap \text{CS}) = \text{EM})$, since MP and CS have no pairs in common (if x is father of y then x is not cousin of y, and vice versa), and also that $(\text{FCS} \subset \text{CS})$, since every pair in FCS will also be a pair in CS (if x is first cousin of y then x is cousin of y). But $(\text{FCS} \neq \text{CS})$ because it is not the case that $(\text{CS} \subset \text{FCS})$. These few illustrative remarks will indicate how relational statements are formulated in set-theoretical terms, and further examples will appear as we proceed.

Up to this point we have been stressing some of the resemblances of sets of ordered pairs to those other sets mentioned in §1, but now we shall begin to develop some of the set-theoretical concepts that are special to relations. Preliminary to this, however, it will be useful to mention an unofficial but pictorially suggestive way to represent sets of ordered pairs by *arrow diagrams*. We can, as we have seen, designate relations by enumerating their ordered pairs within curly brackets. Thus, if z is the relation whose sole member is the ordered pair $(x;y)$ then z is $\{(x;y)\}$. But we can designate z in still another way by writing:

$$x \overset{z}{\rightarrow} y$$

in which x is shown by the labeled arrow to be z-paired with y. In similar fashion, a relation w whose sole members are the pairs $(x;y)$ and $(x;z)$ may be designated by:

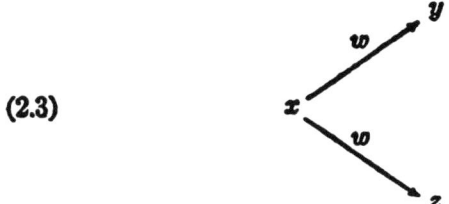

(2.3)

in which x is shown w-paired with y and also with z.

We shall use arrow diagrams in the manner of (2.3) at frequent intervals, hereafter. As a matter of fact, it will be quite convenient to specify a purely abstract set of ordered pairs right now and to construct a diagram of it for future reference. Let us call this hypothetical relation 'ab,' and define it as follows:

(2.4) $(\mathbf{ab} = \{(x_0;x_1), (x_0;x_2), (x_1;x_3), (x_1;x_4), (x_1;x_5), (x_2;x_6),$
$(x_2;x_7), (x_2;x_8), (x_2;x_9)\})$.

This definition specifies **ab** as a relation having just nine ordered pairs. It is easy, with the help of (2.4), to construct a diagram (2.5) in which the structure of **ab** can be seen almost at a glance.

(2.5) **ab**

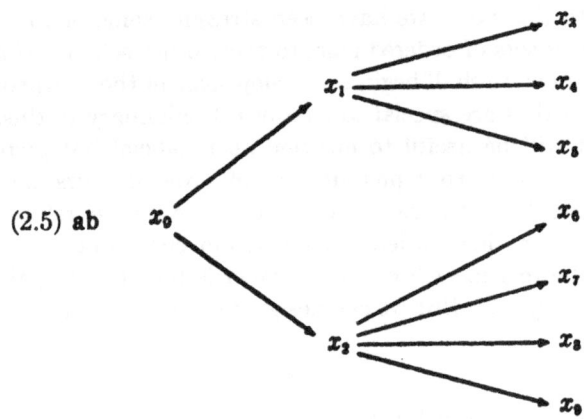

In this diagram the arrows are left unlabeled for the sake of simplicity.

We must now turn to the special concepts that were mentioned a couple of paragraphs back. The first of these is the notion of the *converse* of a relation. The converse $\breve{z}$ of a relation z is the relation to which any ordered pair $(x;y)$ belongs just in case its reverse $(y;x)$ belongs to z:

(2.6) $(\breve{z} =$ the relation in which any ordered pair $(x;y)$ is a member if and only if $((y;x) \ \epsilon \ z))$.

Thus y bears z-converse to x if and only if x bears z to y. For example, if z is the relation of parent to child, then $\breve{z}$ is the relation of child to parent; if z is the relation of host to parasite, then $\breve{z}$ is the relation of parasite to host; if z is the relation of motor neurone to sensory neurone, then $\breve{z}$ is the relation of sensory neurone to motor neurone; and so on. Obviously, the method of arrow diagrams is available for the representation of the converses of sets of ordered pairs. In the next diagram, **ab**-converse, or **ăb**, is represented and the diagram shows not the nine pairs of **ab**, but their nine reverses.

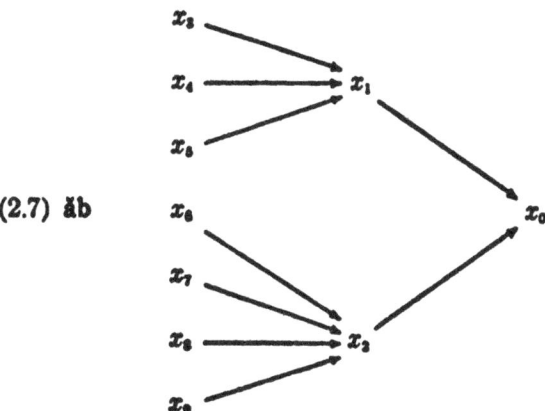

(2.7) **ăb**

The next concept is slightly more difficult. The *image* of a set x by a relation z, briefly $z \,``\, x$, is the set of all first constituents of pairs in z whose second constituents are members of x:

(2.8)   ($z \,``\, x =$ the set in which any y is a member if and only if there is a w such that $((y;w) \,\epsilon\, z)$ and $(w \,\epsilon\, x)$).

For instance, if z is the relation between parasite and host, and x is the set of all mammals, then $z \,``\, x$, the z-image of x, is the set of all parasites of mammals. Similarly, if z is the relation of pupil to teacher, and x is the set of all taxonomists, then the z-image of x is the set of all pupils of taxonomists. Again, if z is **ab** and x is the set whose sole members are x_1 and x_2, then the **ab**-image of x is the set whose sole member is x_0, or, in brief, (**ab** "$\{x_1,x_2\} = \{x_0\}$).

When the ordered pairs in a relation z can be enumerated, as in the case of **ab**, there is a systematic procedure for finding the z-image of any set x:

(2.8)   To find z " x, list all pairs in z whose second constituents are members of x. The set whose members are all *first* constituents of such pairs is the z-image of the set x.

Of course, it may turn out that (z " x = EM), for there may be no z-pairs whose second constituents are members of x. For instance, (**ab** " $\{x_0\}$ = EM).

The notion of image is an extremely versatile and powerful one, and there are several special cases that must now be attended to.

The first of these is quite obvious. The *z-converse image* of a set x, or $\breve{z}$ " x, is simply the set of all first constituents of pairs in z-converse whose second constituents are members of x. For example, if $\breve{z}$ is the relation of child to parent and x is the set of all poets, then $\breve{z}$ " x is the set of all children of poets. Similarly, if $\breve{z}$ is the relation of prey to predator and x is the set of all carnivores, then $\breve{z}$ " x is the set of things preyed upon by carnivores. An abstract instance may be cited by reference to the diagram of **ab**-converse. If $\breve{z}$ is taken as $\breve{a}b$ and x is taken as $\{x_1,x_2\}$, then $\breve{z}$ " x is $\{x_3,x_4,x_5,x_6,x_7,x_8,x_9\}$, i.e., ($\breve{a}b$ " $\{x_1,x_2\} = \{x_3,x_4,x_5,x_6,x_7,x_8,x_9\}$).

When the pairs of a relation z are enumerable, a paraphrasis of (2.8) will tell us how to find the $\breve{z}$-image of any set x:

(2.9)   To find $\breve{z}$ " x, list all pairs in $\breve{z}$ whose second constituents are members of x. The set of all *first* constituents of such pairs is the z-converse image of x.

Of course, a z-converse image may turn out to be empty, as, for instance, ăb " $\{x_4, x_7\}$.

The z-image of the universal set, i.e., z " UN, is called the *domain* of z. It is the set of all first constituents of pairs in z whose second constituents are members of UN—in other words, it is simply the set of all first constituents of pairs in z. Thus, if z is the relation between son and father, then z " UN is the set of all sons; if z is the relation between predator and prey, then z " UN is the set of all predators. There is a handy rule for finding the domain of a relation z by consulting its diagram, if there is one:

(2.10)   To find z " UN, list all objects whose designations stand at the *nocks* of arrows in the diagram of z. The set of all such objects is the domain of z.

Application of this rule to the diagram of **ab**, for instance, will reveal that (**ab** " UN $= \{x_0, x_1, x_2\}$).

The *converse domain* of a relation z is merely the z-converse image of the universal set, i.e., $\breve{z}$ " UN. If z is the relation of killer to victim, then (since $\breve{z}$ is the relation of victim to killer) $\breve{z}$ " UN is the set of all victims of killers. Similarly, if z is the relation of artery to vein, then (since $\breve{z}$ is the relation of vein to artery) $\breve{z}$ " UN is the set of all veins. An obvious paraphrasis of the diagram-rule for domains yields one for converse domains:

(2.11)   To find $\breve{z}$ " UN, list all objects whose designations stand at the *nocks* of arrows in the diagram of $\breve{z}$. The set of all such objects is the converse domain of z.

(It will be apparent that this is also the set of objects whose designations stand at the *heads* of arrows in the diagram of z.) Applying this rule to the diagram of ăb, we can easily discover that (ăb " UN $= \{x_3, x_4, x_5, x_6, x_7, x_8, x_9, x_1, x_2\}$).

Let us now make use of these special cases of image to master certain further set-theoretical concepts having to do with relations.

The *field* of a relation z is the set of all first constituents of z-pairs together with all first constituents of $\breve{z}$-pairs. Since the set of all first constituents of z-pairs is z " UN and the set of all first constituents of $\breve{z}$-pairs is $\breve{z}$ " UN, the field of z is simply the sum (1.14) of its domain and its converse domain, i.e., the field of z is (z " UN $\cup$ $\breve{z}$ " UN). For example, if z is the relation of parasite to host, then the field of z is the set in which all parasites and also all hosts of parasites are members. Again, if z is the relation of nucleus to chromosome, then the field of z is the set in which all nuclei and also all chromosomes are members. For those who are still relying upon diagrams, there is a simple rule for discovering the field of a relation z, provided that a diagram of z or of $\breve{z}$ is available:

(2.13)   To find (z " UN $\cup$ $\breve{z}$ " UN), simply list all those objects whose designations appear at the *nocks* of arrows in the diagram of z or of $\breve{z}$, and also those whose designations appear at the *heads* of arrows. The set of all these objects is the field of z.

Applying this rule to the diagram of **ab** (or of **ăb**) it will be found that ((**ab** " UN $\cup$ **ăb** " UN) = $\{x_0, x_1, x_2, x_3, x_4, x_5, x_6, x_7, x_8, x_9\}$). It should be obvious that the field of a relation is also the field of its converse.

It is very often useful to have some way to designate a relation whose domain is restricted to some given set. Consider, for example, a relation z and a set x, and then imagine the relation z' in which any pair is a member just in case it is a z-pair and its first constituent is a member of x. Every pair in z' will thus be a z-pair, and each member of the domain of z will be a member of x. We will call z' 'z with its domain limited to x' or, briefly, '$(x \mid z)$.' Put more formally:

(2.13) $((x \mid z)$ = the relation in which any pair $(w;u)$ is a member if and only if $(w \in x)$ and $((w;u) \in z))$.

Examples: Let z be the relation between parent and child, and let x be the set of centenarians. Then $(x \restriction z)$ is the relation between centenarian parent and child. Let z be the relation between parasite and host and let x be the set of arachnids. Then $(x \restriction z)$ is the relation between any parasitic arachnid and its host. The diagram of **ab** will furnish a final example. Let z be **ab** and let x be $\{x_0\}$. Then $(x \restriction z)$ will be the relation between x_0 and x_1, and also between x_0 and x_2. For, clearly, $(x_0 \; \epsilon \; \{x_0\})$, and $((x_0 ; x_1) \; \epsilon \; \textbf{ab})$, and also $((x_0 ; x_2) \; \epsilon \; \textbf{ab})$.

In a closely similar manner, we can specify $(z \restriction y)$ as the relation z with its *converse domain* limited to a set y, in accordance with the following rule:

(2.14) $((z \restriction y) =$ the relation in which any pair $(w;u)$ is a member if and only if $((w;u) \; \epsilon \; z)$ and $(u \; \epsilon \; y))$.

$(z \restriction y)$ is, therefore, the relation to which any z-pair belongs just in case its second constituent is a member of y. If, for instance, z is the relation between hunter and quarry, and y is the set of all birds, then $(z \restriction y)$ is the relation between hunter and avian quarry. Similarly, if z is the relation between husband and wife, and y is the set of all snobs, then $(z \restriction y)$ is the relation between husband and snobbish wife. Pairs in this relation are not uncommon. Furthermore—referring now to the diagram of **ab**—it may be seen that $(\textbf{ab} \restriction \{x_6\})$ is a relation that holds exclusively between x_2 and x_6.

The import of '$(x \restriction z \restriction y)$' should be obvious: it designates the set of all z-pairs whose first constituent is a member of x and whose second constituent is a member of y, i.e., z with its domain limited to x and its converse domain limited to y:

(2.15) $((x \restriction z \restriction y) =$ the relation in which any pair $(w;u)$ is a member if and only if $(w \; \epsilon \; x)$ and $((w;u) \; \epsilon \; z)$ and $(u \; \epsilon \; y))$.

Examples: If x is the set of all postmasters, and z is the relation between father and son, and y is the set of all embryologists, then $(x \uparrow z \upharpoonright y)$ is the relation between postmaster father and embryologist son. If x is the set of all cats, and z is the hunter-quarry relation, and y is the set of all reptiles, then $(x \uparrow z \upharpoonright y)$ is the relation between feline hunter and reptilian quarry. This latter relation may possibly be empty. Finally, it should be easy to see, by looking at the diagram of **ab**, that $(\{x_2\} \uparrow \textbf{ab} \upharpoonright \{x_9\})$ is a relation exclusively between x_2 and x_9.

When both the domain and the converse domain of a relation z are to be restricted to the same set x, a convenient notation is provided by the following rule:

(2.16) $((z \restriction x) = (x \uparrow z \upharpoonright x))$.

To give a single example, if z is the relation between master and slave, and x is the set of Aztecs, then $(z \restriction x)$ is the relation between Aztec master and Aztec slave.

Our next step will be to define a relation of special importance for our projected treatment of taxonomic systems. This relation will be called 'B,' and it will be introduced by the following rule:

(2.17)   (B = the relation in which any pair $(x;z)$ is a member
              if and only if $(x \, \epsilon \, (z \text{ `` UN } \cap \, \breve{z} \text{ `` UN})))$.

This rule *looks* a little complicated: actually, it is quite easy to understand. It was pointed out in the preceding section that to say '$(x \, \epsilon \, (y \cap \bar{z})$' is just to say that x is a member of y but not of z. Hence, to say that $(x \, \epsilon \, (z \text{ `` UN } \cap \, \breve{z} \text{ `` UN}))$ is merely to assert that x is a member of the domain of z but *not* of the converse domain of z. Therefore, the rule above is telling us in effect that any ordered pair $(x;z)$ is such that $((x;z) \, \epsilon \, B)$ just in case x is in the domain, but not in the converse domain, of z.

Let us look at the diagram of **ab**, for example, and try to discover what B-pairs are represented therein. Now, it is obvious that x_0 is the only member of the domain of **ab** that is not also a member of the converse domain of **ab**; for x_0 is the only first constituent of **ab**-pairs that is not also the second constituent of some **ab**-pair. Hence $(x_0;$**ab**$)$ is the only B-pair represented in the diagram of **ab**.

On the other hand, if we examine the diagram of **ăb** we shall find six B-pairs. For $x_3, x_4, \ldots, x_9$ all are first constituents, but not second constituents, of **ăb**-pairs; hence, $x_3, x_4, \ldots, x_9$ all are in the domain, but not in the converse domain, of **ăb**; hence, $(x_3;$**ăb**$), (x_4;$**ăb**$), \ldots, (x_9;$**ăb**$)$ all are B-pairs.

Some intuitive flavor to this discussion may be added by reading '$((x;z) \in B)$' as 'x is a *beginner* of the relation z.' The *set* of all beginners of a relation z is simply the set of all first constituents of B-pairs whose second constituent is z. But this set is the B-image of $\{z\}$. Hence, B " $\{z\}$ is the set of all beginners of z. B " $\{$**ăb**$\}$, for example, has six members: $x_3, x_4, \ldots, x_9$. But B " $\{$**ab**$\}$ has only one member: x_0. We might, therefore, call x_0 '*the* beginner of **ab**.' This last remark, concerning the use of the definite article 'the,' brings up a rather important point that will now be explained.

For some choices of x and z it may happen that the z-image of $\{x\}$ has exactly one member. For instance, if z is the relation of father to child, and x is Charles Darwin, then, of course, z " $\{x\}$ has only one member—namely, Erasmus Darwin. Similarly, if z is the relation of mother to child and x is Abraham Lincoln, then z " $\{x\}$ has exactly one member—namely, Nancy Hanks Lincoln. In general, when there is a unique y such that $(y \in z$ " $\{x\})$, then we may significantly speak of *the* z of x: it is in this way that we use the phrase '*the* father of Charles Darwin' and the phrase '*the* mother of Abraham Lincoln.' Thus, using 'z ' x' as shorthand for 'the (one) z of x,' we may adopt the following convention:

(2.18) $(z$ ' x = the unique y such that $(y \in z$ " $\{x\}))$.

Hence, if MP is the relation of father to child and FP is the relation of mother to child, we have (Erasmus Darwin =

MP ' Charles Darwin) and also (Nancy Hanks Lincoln = FP ' Abraham Lincoln). Similarly, by consulting the diagram of **ab** it will be seen, for example, that $(x_0 = \textbf{ab} \,{}^{\backprime}\, x_1)$ and also that $(x_0 = \textbf{ab} \,{}^{\backprime}\, x_2)$. When z " $\{x\}$ is empty, or contains *more* than one member, then there will be no unique y such that $(y = z \,{}^{\backprime}\, x)$. Thus, if P is the relation of parent to child, it is not significant to use expression 'P ' x,' for if P" $\{x\}$ has any members at all, it has at least two.

In like vein (as already suggested) we may call x_0 '*the* beginner of **ab**,' i.e. $(\text{B} \,{}^{\backprime}\, \textbf{ab} = x_0)$. But, since there are six beginners of **ab**-converse, it is quite plain that 'B ' **ăb**' designates nothing at all.

Using this new notation, we shall adopt an abbreviation that may be employed whenever it is useful to do so:

(2.19) $(\text{FIELD} \,{}^{\backprime}\, z = (z \text{ " UN} \cup \breve{z} \text{ " UN)})$.

Clearly, 'FIELD ' z' may be read 'the field of (the relation) z.'

We must now undertake to explain what is meant by the *relative product* $(x \mid y)$ of a relation x and a relation y.

(2.20) $((x \mid y) =$ the relation in which any pair $(w;v)$ is a member if and only if there is some u such that $((w;u) \,\epsilon\, x)$ and $((u;v) \,\epsilon\, y))$.

Thus, w will bear $(x \mid y)$ to v just in case w bears x to something u that bears y to v. For example, let x be the relation of brother to sibling and y be the relation of parent to child. Then $(x \mid y)$ is the relation of uncle to nephew or neice. For if there is a u such that w is brother of u and u is parent of v then w is uncle of v. It should be noted that we may form the relative product of a relation with itself. Thus, if x is the relation of parasite to host, then w will bear $(x \mid x)$ to v just in case w parasitizes something u that in turn parasitizes v, i.e., just when w is a parasite of a parasite of v. Furthermore, it should be pointed out that we can construct relative-product designations having any number of strokes. For instance if x is the relation of employer to employee, y is the relation of killer to victim, and z is the relation of husband to wife, then $(x \mid y \mid z)$ is the relation in which w stands to v when w is the employer of someone who kills someone who is husband of v. Similarly, if x is the relation of parent to child, then $(x \mid x \mid x \mid x)$ is the relation of great-great-grandparent to great-great-grandchild. Some illustrations of relative product may also be obtained by looking at the diagram of **ab**. For there we shall see that x_0 bears $(\mathbf{ab} \mid \mathbf{ab})$ to each of $x_3, x_4, \ldots, x_9$. Furthermore, by consulting the sketch of **ab**-converse, we shall see that each of $x_3, x_4, \ldots, x_9$ bears $(\mathbf{\breve{a}b} \mid \mathbf{\breve{a}b})$ to x_0.

We can now easily understand the notion of the *proper ancestral* z_{p0} of a relation z:

(2.21) $(z_{p0} =$ the relation in which any pair $(x;y)$ is a member if and only if $((x;y) \ \epsilon \ z)$ or $((x;y) \ \epsilon \ (z \mid z))$ or $((x;y) \ \epsilon$ $(z \mid z \mid z))$ or $((x;y) \ \epsilon \ (z \mid z \mid z \mid z))$ or $\ldots)$.

(The reader may carry out this sequence as far as he pleases). For example: if z is the relation of parent to child, then $((x;y) \ \epsilon \ z_{p0})$ just in case x is parent of y, or else x is grandparent of y, or else x is great-grandparent of y, or else x is great-great-grandparent of y, or $\ldots$.

When z can be diagramed, there is a convenient rule for discovering all z_{p0}-pairs. When $(x;y)$ is represented by '$x \rightarrow y$' we shall say that the designation of x and the designation of y are one *forward* arrow-step apart. The rule now follows:

(2.22)   To find z_{p0}, list all pairs whose constituent-designations are one forward arrow-step apart, then list all pairs whose constituent designations are two forward arrow-steps apart, then list all pairs whose constituent designations are three forward arrow-steps apart, and so on. The set of all such pairs is the proper ancestral of z.

Applying this rule to the diagram of **ab**, we shall find that there are sixteen ordered pairs in $\mathbf{ab}_{po}$:

$$(\mathbf{ab}_{po} = \{(x_0;x_1), (x_0;x_2), (x_1;x_3), (x_1;x_4), (x_1;x_5), (x_2;x_6), (x_2;x_7),$$
$$(x_2;x_8), (x_2;x_9), (x_0;x_3), (x_0;x_4), (x_0;x_5), (x_0;x_6), (x_0;x_7), (x_0;x_8),$$
$$(x_0;x_9)\}).$$

Similarly, we should find that $\mathbf{\breve{a}b}_{po}$ has sixteen pairs; also, they will be the reverses of the pairs in $\mathbf{ab}_{po}$. Hence:

$$(\mathbf{\breve{a}b}_{po} = \{(x_1;x_0), (x_2;x_0), \ldots, (x_9;x_0)\}).$$

If we add the condition '$(x = y)$' to the right-hand side of (2.21) we shall specify another relation called the *ancestral* of z, or briefly, $*z$:

(2.23)   ($*z$ = the relation in which any pair $(x;y)$ is a member if and only if $(x = y)$ or $((x;y) \ \epsilon \ z_{po})$)

Thus, $*\mathbf{ab}$ is a relation with twenty-six pairs: the sixteen in $\mathbf{ab}_{po}$ together with ten more obtained by pairing each member of the field of **ab** with itself: $(x_0;x_0), (x_1;x_1), \cdots, (x_9;x_9)$. Analogous remarks hold for $*\mathbf{\breve{a}b}$.

Next, we shall explain what is intended by saying that a relation z belongs to the set of *one-many* relations, designated by 'One–Many':

(2.24)   (($z \ \epsilon$ One-Many) if and only if, for all x, all w, and all y if $((x;w) \ \epsilon \ z)$ and $((y;w) \ \epsilon \ z)$ then $(x = y)$).

The central idea of (2.24) is this: if z is one-many and w is any member of its field, then *not more* than one thing will bear z to w. For example, **ab** is a member of One-Many: a glance at its diagram will show that each member of its field is the second constituent of at most one **ab**-pair. But, **ab**-converse is not one-many: x_2, e.g., is the second constituent of *four* $\mathbf{\breve{a}b}$-pairs. Obviously, $\mathbf{\breve{a}b}$ is many-one:

(2.25) $((z \ \epsilon \ \text{Many-One})$ if and only if, for all w, all x, and all y, if $((w;x) \ \epsilon \ z)$ and $((w;y) \ \epsilon \ z)$ then $(x = y))$.

Hence, in a many-one relation, no member of its field can be the first constituent of more than one pair. As we have mentioned, **ăb** is such a relation; but **ab** is not.

Finally, the set of one-one relations is defined as follows:

(2.26) $((z \ \epsilon \ \text{One-One})$ if and only if $(z \ \epsilon \ \text{One-Many})$ and also $(z \ \epsilon \ \text{Many-One}))$.

In such a relation, each member of its field is the first constituent of at most one pair and the second constituent of at most one pair.

3. Hierarchies

We come now to relations called *hierarchies* or *hierarchical relations*. As a class, these have hardly attracted the attention of logicians. But they are exemplified in biology so frequently as to have been made the object of special investigation by a biologist, J. H. Woodger (1937, 1952). The following account of hierarchies is heavily indebted to Woodger's studies.

Hierarchies are generated by familiar biological processes. Imagine, for example, a cell that divides into two others, each of which divides into two further cells that in their turn divide into still others—and so on: the well-known branching diagrams of cell lineages are pictorial representations of hierarchies generated by such cell divisions. Similar diagrams are also used to represent the splitting of some initially chosen set of objects into two or more subsets, which are in turn split into smaller subsets, and so on, or to represent the distribution of authority in a business organization. Woodger has been able to specify, in set-theoretical terms, what it is that such diagrams share in common; so that diagrams may be dispensed with (except for illustrative purposes) in favor of a notation more favorable for calculating and for methodological discourse in general.

Using 'HR' to designate the set of all hierarchies (hierarchical relations) we now present Woodger's 1952 definition:

(3.1)   (HR = the set in which any relation z is a member
          if and only if ($z \in$ One-Many) and ($\breve{z}$ " UN =
          $\breve{z}_{po}$ " {B ' z})).

According to this definition, a hierarchy is any one-many relation z whose converse domain is identical with the set of all *first* constituents of $\check{z}_{po}$-pairs whose *second* constituent is the beginner of z. Let us apply these criteria to **ab**. We have seen (page 24) that **ab** is a member of One-Many, so it meets the first requirement. Next, we must see whether its converse domain is identical with the $\check{a}b_{po}$-image of the set whose sole member is its beginner. Now, we know that **ab** has a unique beginner, (page 22), namely, x_0. Furthermore, we know that the converse domain of **ab** is $\{x_1, x_2, \ldots, x_9\}$ (page 17). Next, by consulting the diagram of **ab**-converse, and picking out all $\check{a}b_{po}$-pairs whose second constituent is x_0 (see the list sketched on page 24), and then picking out all *first* constituents of such pairs, we again obtain the set $\{x_1, x_2, \ldots, x_9\}$. Hence, the converse domain of **ab** and the $\check{a}b_{po}$-image of $\{B\,{}^{\backprime}\,\mathbf{ab}\}$ are identical, and so **ab** satisfies the second criterion, also. Therefore, **ab** is a hierarchy, i.e., (**ab** ϵ HR).

On the other hand, **ab**-converse satisfies neither criterion. It is not one-many, and it has no *unique* beginner. Consequently, under the adopted rules, **ab**-converse is not a hierarchy.

Among other matters connected with the general theory of hierarchies, Woodger has carefully explicated the notion of the *levels* of a hierarchical relation. Let us now see how he has accomplished this. The first item that needs explaining is what is meant by the *interval* between two members x and y of the field of a relation z, or, briefly, the z-interval between x and y, or, even more briefly, $z\,(x \longmapsto y)$:

(3.2) $(z\,(x \longmapsto y) =$ the set in which any w is a member if and only if $(w\,\epsilon\,(*\check{z}\,{}^{\backprime\backprime}\,\{x\}\,\cap\,*z\,{}^{\backprime\backprime}\,\{y\})))$.

Thus, w will be a member of $z\,(x \longmapsto y)$ just in case w is the first constituent of a $*\check{z}$-pair whose second constituent is x and *also* w is the first constituent of a $*z$-pair whose second constituent is y.

If z is diagramed then the following rule can be used to find z-intervals:

(3.3)   To find z $(x \longmapsto y)$: (1) If $(x = y)$ and no arrow chain
         connects the designation of x with that of y then
         z $(x \longmapsto y)$ is simply $\{x\}$ or $\{y\}$. (2) Otherwise, list
         all members of the field of z (including x and y) whose
         designations lie in some chain of arrows linking the
         designation of x with that of y. The set of all such
         members of the field of z is the z-interval between,
         and inclusive of, x and y.

Applying this rule to the diagram of **ab**, it is easy to discover
that (among others) all of the following statements are true:

$$\textbf{ab } (x_0 \longmapsto x_0) = \{x_0\}),$$
$$\textbf{ab } (x_0 \longmapsto x_2) = \{x_0,x_2\}),$$
$$\textbf{ab } (x_0 \longmapsto x_6) = \{x_0,x_2,x_6\}),$$
$$\textbf{ab } (x_1 \longmapsto x_3) = \{x_1,x_3\}),$$
$$\textbf{ab } (x_1 \longmapsto x_9) = \text{EM}).$$

Next, we shall define a relation z_n that holds between x and y
when z $(x \longmapsto y)$ has exactly $n + 1$ members. Using '$(\text{N} (z (x \longmapsto y))$
$= n + 1)$' to mean that the z-interval between x and y has
$n + 1$ members we put:

(3.4) $(z_n$ = the relation in which any ordered pair $(x;y)$ is a
         member if and only if n is an integer (≥ 0) and
         $(\text{N} (z (x \longmapsto y)) = n + 1))$.

In purely diagrammatic terms, $(x;y)$ will be a member of z_n
just in case there are n arrows in the chain of arrows linking
up the designation of x with that of y. Clearly, $((x_0;x_0) \; \epsilon \; \textbf{ab}_0)$,
$((x_0;x_9) \; \epsilon \; \textbf{ab}_2)$ and $((x_2;x_7) \; \epsilon \; \textbf{ab}_1)$.

Now we are ready to explain what is meant by the nth level
of a hierarchy. Using 'LEV_n ' z' to mean the nth level of z:

(3.5)   (LEV$_n$ ' z = the set in which any x is a member if
and only if ((B ' $z;x$) ϵ z_n) and (z ϵ HR)).

Or, in pictorial terms, the nth level of a hierarchy z is the set of
all those objects whose designations can be reached (in a diagram
of z) by going exactly n forward arrow-steps from the designation
of the beginner of z. It is discoverable at once, by reference to
the diagram of **ab**, for instance, that (LEV$_0$ ' **ab** = $\{x_0\}$), that
(LEV$_1$ ' **ab** = $\{x_1,x_2\}$) and that (LEV$_2$ ' **ab** = $\{x_3, x_4, \ldots, x_9\}$).
Thus, **ab** is a hierarchy with three levels.

Finally, we can define the set LEV " $\{z\}$ of all levels of a
hierarchy z as the set of those x's such that, for some n, x is the
nth level of z:

(3.6)   (LEV " $\{z\}$ = the set in which any x is a member if
and only if there is an n such that (x = LEV$_n$ ' z)).

With this definition we conclude our account of Woodger's
treatment of hierarchies, and we shall turn, in the next section,
to taxonomic matters.

4. An Introduction to Taxonomic Systems

Taxonomy, without a doubt, is an extremely complicated business, and it shares with other sciences the characteristic that it cannot be practiced by mere rote. It is never possible, for example, to guarantee the success of a taxonomic research program by setting down antecedent directives that are then to be followed out step by step until the requisite discoveries have been made. Taxonomic inquiry, like any other serious investigative activity, requires the persistent exercise of creative imagination and intelligence. But, wholly aside from those most general standards of excellence to which the sciences at large aspire, the pursuit of taxonomy presupposes the acceptance of a few more or less conventional rules, and among these are some that prescribe the general form into which any taxonomic classificatory system is to be cast.

By general consent, taxonomists regard the celebrated eighteenth-century Swedish botanist Carolus Linnaeus as having been the first to enunciate and exploit on an extensive scale rules that are similar to ones now regulating taxonomic classification. (It is worth mentioning that perhaps the chief contribution of Linnaeus to taxonomic methodology was the formulation of a most elaborate set of regulations governing the introduction of taxonomic group names into the vocabulary of the science.) From the very beginnings of the science of biological classifying it has been the custom to generate taxonomic systems by selecting some set of organisms and repeatedly subdividing it on the basis of specifically stated membership criteria. But, until Linnaeus' time it was not invariably the case that the resulting subsets—from now on we shall call them *taxonomic groups*—themselves became the object of classificatory attention. Since the time of Linnaeus, however, taxonomists have come to regard as taxonomic groups only those sets of organisms that have been assigned to membership in some *taxonomic category* of taxonomic groups. Hence, each organism classified in neo-Linnaean systems is a member of several taxonomic groups each of which is in turn a member of some taxonomic category.

At present, there are seven principal categories to which taxonomic groups may belong: Kingdom, Phylum (in zoology) or Division (in botany), Class, Order, Family, Genus, and Species. These are sometimes called "obligatory" categories, in the sense that a specification of the taxonomic affiliations of any organism will at minimum consist in listing its membership in some taxonomic group in each of these seven sets of taxonomic groups. To illustrate this point, each modern human occupies a place in the taxonomic scheme of things that is minimally specified as follows (the names to the right of the colons are taxonomic group names):

(4.1)   Kingdom : Animalia

Phylum : Chordata

Class : Mammalia

Order : Primates

Family : Hominidae

Genus : *Homo*

Species : *Homo sapiens*

Similarly, each honey bee is taxonomically affiliated as follows:

(4.2)   Kingdom : Animalia
                Phylum : Arthropoda
                    Class : Insecta
                        Order : Hymenoptera
                            Family : Apidae
                                Genus : *Apis*
                                    Species : *Apis mellifera*

Such classifications, of course, are relative to some taxonomic system: in both of the above cases, a system in which the animal kingdom is split into several phyla (of which Chordata and Arthropoda are only two) each of which in turn is split into several classes (e.g., Chordata into Mammalia and several others and Arthropoda into Insecta and several others) each of which in *its* turn is split into several orders (e.g., Mammalia into Primates and others and Insecta into Hymenoptera and others) —and so on. Systems with which none but the seven principal categories are associated, however, are only referred to when but a rough indication of the taxonomic status of an organism is desired. For, more often than not, a detailed study of the organisms belonging to some taxonomic group will result in the production of a classificatory system with which are associated a good many other categories besides principal ones. A single example will suffice to illustrate this point. A recent taxonomic study of mammals (Simpson, 1945) resulted in a classificatory system with groups in each of the following categories: Class, Subclass, Infraclass, Cohort, Superorder, Order, Suborder, Infraorder, Superfamily, Family, Subfamily, Tribe, Subtribe, and Genus. (Categories precedent to Class and subsequent to Genus are left tacit in this system.) Relative to this classification, therefore, the taxonomic status of each human is expressed as follows:

(4.3)   Class : Mammalia
                Subclass : Theria
                    Infraclass : Eutheria
                        Cohort : Unguiculata
                            Order : Primates
                                Suborder : Anthropoidea
                                    Superfamily : Hominoidea
                                        Family : Hominidae
                                            Genus : *Homo*

(It so happens that in Simpson's treatment there are no sub-families, tribes, or subtribes of hominids.) Supplementary additions of this kind, however, do not *indefinitely* expand the taxonomic vocabulary of category names, for a given system will rarely presuppose more than twenty, and two otherwise distantly related systems may have precisely the same associated categories. Yet it is noteworthy that restraint upon the multiplication of categories has not greatly *over*simplified the taxonomic enterprise. Simpson's classification of mammals mentions 2,864 genera of mammals, and recent well-known estimates place the number of animal species alone at well in excess of a million. These large numbers are indicative of the immensity of the labors to whose completion taxonomists have set themselves.

Roughly speaking then, a taxonomic system is a structure obtainable by successively partitioning some initial set of organisms into subsets each of which belongs to some taxonomic category. In the sequel we shall undertake to give formal expression to this claim; and with an eye to this development we shall now lay down some conventions, heretofore implicit, that will govern our further use of taxonomic group names and taxonomic category names. We shall construe taxonomic group names— 'Insecta,' 'Primates,' *'Homo sapiens,'* 'Arthropoda,' and the rest—as set names, one and all, i.e., as names of sets of organisms.

For we shall wish to regard the expression '(Gargantua ϵ Primates),' for example, as a set-theoretical formulation of the statement that Gargantua belongs to the taxonomic group Primates. Hence, if any group name appears to the right of 'ϵ' in a set-membership statement, then only the name of an individual—'Smith,' 'Jones,' 'Bushman,' 'Tom Fool,' 'Lassie'—can significantly appear to the left. If no names for certain individuals are at hand, then they must be manufactured. Now, this decision is not made on the grounds that taxonomic groups 'really are' sets of organisms: it is made solely for the reason that by making it we can bring statements about taxonomic groups within the scope of the systematized and precise idioms of set-theory, with all of the advantages this carries. Those who wish to put forward other interpretations of taxonomic group names are, of course, free to do so (see, for example, Woodger, 1951 and 1952). In the same purely methodological spirit we shall construe category names—'Kingdom,' 'Phylum,' 'Class,' 'Order,' and so on—as names of sets of taxonomic groups, hence, as names of sets of sets of organisms. For we shall wish such an expression as '(*Homo sapiens* ϵ Species)' to count as a set-theoretical version of the claim that *Homo sapiens* belongs to the category Species. Hence, if any such category name appears to the right of 'ϵ' in a set-membership statement, then only a name designating a set of individuals (a taxonomic group name, for example) can significantly appear to the left. Thus '(Primates ϵ Order),' '(Insecta ϵ Class),' '(*Homo* ϵ Phylum)' all are statements (the third of which is simply false); but such expressions as '(Gargantua ϵ Suborder)' and '(Gregor Mendel ϵ Genus)' are not to be counted as statements at all. These syntactical remarks are directly in line with those made near the beginning of §1. Organism names belong to the name group N^1; taxonomic group names belong to the name group N^2; taxonomic category names belong to the name group N^3.

Furthermore, the discussion to follow will be greatly facilitated by having at hand some illustrative material in the form of an actual taxonomic classificatory system. Published systems are all rather too large to be useful for our purposes, but it will turn out that nothing is lost by selecting representative *parts* of such systems and centering our discussion about these. In particular, we have chosen a fragment of Simpson's classification of mammals, to which reference has already been made:

(4.4)   Order : Primates

Suborder : Prosimii

Infraorder : Lemuriformes

Superfamily : Tupaioidea

Superfamily : Lemuroidea

Superfamily : Daubentonioidea

Infraorder : Lorisiformes

Infraorder : Tarsiiformes

Suborder : Anthropoidea

Superfamily : Ceboidea

Superfamily : Cercopithecoidea

Superfamily : Hominoidea

This example is complete, as far as it goes. In Simpson's system, the order Primates is divided into exactly two suborders. The first suborder, Prosimii, is divided into three infraorders, of which the first contains three superfamilies, and the second and third none. The second suborder, Anthropoidea, contains no infraorders, but is split directly by Simpson into three superfamilies. Thus we have a minute taxonomic system of twelve taxonomic groups: one order, two suborders, three infraorders, and six superfamilies.

Some preliminary abbreviatory conventions will save us much

writing, later on. Let us agree to abbreviate the names of taxonomic groups in our example as follows:

(4.5)   'G_0' for 'Primates'
            'G_1' for 'Prosimii'
            'G_2' for 'Anthropoidea'
            'G_3' for 'Lemuriformes'
            'G_4' for 'Lorisiformes'
            'G_5' for 'Tarsiiformes'
            'G_6' for 'Ceboidea'
            'G_7' for 'Cercopithecoidea'
            'G_8' for 'Hominoidea'
            'G_9' for 'Tupaioidea'
            'G_{10}' for 'Lemuroidea'
            'G_{11}' for 'Daubentonioidea'

Furthermore, let us adopt a name for the *set* of all these groups:

(4.6) $(S = \{G_0, G_1, \ldots, G_{11}\})$.

Recalling the conventions about group and category names, it will be seen that each member of S is a member of some category, and that each member of a member of S is an organism.

Next, let us pair off Primates with each of its suborders, Prosimii with each of its infraorders, Lemuriformes with each of its superfamilies, and Anthropoidea with each of its superfamilies; and let us call the resulting set of eleven ordered pairs of taxonomic groups 'SMP':

(4.7) $(SMP = \{(G_0;G_1), (G_0;G_2), (G_1;G_3), (G_1;G_4), (G_1;G_5),$
            $(G_3;G_9), (G_3;G_{10}), (G_3;G_{11}), (G_2;G_6), (G_2;G_7), (G_2;G_8)\})$.

SMP is thus a relation whose field is S. Let us record this for future reference:

(4.8) $(S = (SMP \text{ `` } UN \cup \check{S}MP \text{ `` } UN))$.

Next, let us construct an arrow diagram of **SMP** and establish some statements about the latter that will be of use to us in the sequel. To this diagram we shall append an indication of the categories to which the groups designated in it belong.

(4.9) SMP

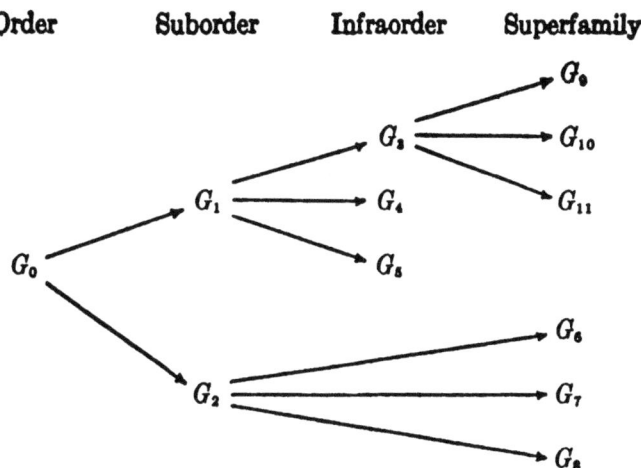

Order	Suborder	Infraorder	Superfamily

From this arrow diagram, certain statements about **SMP** are readily apparent. First of all, it is clearly one-many:

(4.10)   (**SMP** ϵ One-Many)

It has a single beginner, namely, G_0:

(4.11)   (B ' **SMP** = G_0).

Its domain consists of the groups G_0, G_1, ... G_3:

(4.12)   (**SMP** " UN = $\{G_0, G_1, G_2, G_3\}$).

Its converse domain consists of the groups G_1, G_2, ... , G_{11}:

(4.13)   (S$\check{M}$P " UN = $\{G_1, G_2, G_3, G_4, G_5, G_6, G_7, G_8, G_9, G_{10}, G_{11}\}$).

Its field, as already pointed out, is **S**:

(4.14)	((**SMP** " UN ∪ **SM̌P** " UN) = **S**),

or, using the abbreviation mentioned in (2.19):

(4.15)	(FIELD ' **SMP** = **S**).

By imagining all arrows reversed so as to obtain a diagram of **SMP**-converse, it is easy to see that the set of all **SM̌P**$_{po}$-pairs whose second constituent is G_0 is identical with the converse domain of **SMP**, i.e., that:

(4.16)	(**SM̌P** " UN = **SM̌P**$_{po}$ " {B ' **SMP**}).

It follows from this and from (4.10), together with the definition of 'HR,' that **SMP** is a hierarchy:

(4.17)	(**SMP** ε HR)

This last result instantiates a claim that we shall make presently to the effect that all other taxonomic systems are hierarchies also.

   SMP is a hierarchy with just four levels:

(4.18)	(LEV$_0$ ' **SMP** = {G_0}),
	(LEV$_1$ ' **SMP** = {G_1,G_2}),
	(LEV$_2$ ' **SMP** = {G_3,G_4,G_5,G_6,G_7,G_8}),
	(LEV$_3$ ' **SMP** = {G_9,G_{10},G_{11}}).

(The fact that the arrows connecting 'G_2' with 'G_6,' with 'G_7,' and with 'G_8' have been elongated to facilitate the attachment of category designations to the diagram should not lead one to confuse the members of LEV$_2$ ' **SMP** with those of LEV$_3$ ' **SMP**.)

   A further consequence of the definition of **SMP** is the following:

(4.19)	For all x and all y , if ((x;y) ε **SMP**) then ($x \neq y$).

A single example will suffice to illustrate this statement. $(G_0;G_2)$ is a member of **SMP**; and, hence, if G_0 and G_2 were identical, then $(G_2;G_0)$ would also be an **SMP**-pair. But, since $(G_2;G_0)$ is *not* an **SMP**-pair, it follows that $(G_0 \neq G_2)$. (Of course, this is true on taxonomic grounds, as well: (Primates $\neq$ Anthropoidea), for some primates are not anthropoids at all).

A still further consequence of the definition of **SMP** is this:

(4.20)   For all x and all y, if $((x;y) \in \textbf{SMP})$ then there is no z such that $((x;z) \in \textbf{SMP})$ and $((z;y) \in \textbf{SMP})$.

This may be verified by inspecting either the diagram of **SMP** or else the list of **SMP**-pairs.

The next statements about **SMP** cannot be obtained from its definition alone; but they are warranted by knowledge of what this fragment of Simpson's classification is intended to convey.

The first of these states that if a taxonomic group in the field of **SMP** is split into two distinct subgroups, then the latter have no members in common:

(4.21)   For all x, all y, and all z, if $((x;y) \in \textbf{SMP})$ and $((x;z) \in$ **SMP**$)$ and $(y \neq z)$ then $((y \cap z) = \text{EM})$.

For instance: $(G_0;G_1)$ and $(G_0;G_2)$ are both **SMP**-pairs, $(G_1 \neq G_2)$, and (as required) $((G_1 \cap G_2) = \text{EM})$, for nothing is both a prosimian and an anthropoid.

The second of these statements is the claim that if y is one of the groups into which x has been divided then y is always included in x:

(4.22)   For all x and all y, if $((x;y) \in \textbf{SMP})$ then $(y \subset x)$.

Thus, $(G_0;G_1)$ is an **SMP**-pair and $(G_1 \subset G_0)$, for every prosimian is a primate. Furthermore $(G_8 \subset G_0)$, $(G_9 \subset G_1)$, $(G_3 \subset G_0)$, and so on. (4.22) is a formal account of what is expressed with the help of *indentations* when taxonomic systems are being written up.

Finally, we may notice the following:

(4.23)   For all x and all y, if $((x;y) \in \mathbf{SMP})$ then there is no z such that $(z \in \mathbf{S})$ and $(z \neq x)$ and $(z \neq y)$ and $(y \subset z)$ and $(z \subset x)$.

Now, these are by no means all the statements that we are equipped to make about **SMP**. But among them are some that will be useful shortly and they may be at least faintly suggestive of the expressive power that is to be gained by the use of set-theory to describe particular taxonomic systems. Now let us begin to discuss taxonomic systems in greater generality.

5. The Structure of Taxonomic Systems

In this section we shall undertake to construct an account of taxonomic systems in general. This will require a basic vocabulary consisting of only two biological signs in addition to the various notations of set-theory and aside from the expressions occurring in purely illustrative material. These two signs are introduced in the following rules:

(5.1)   The sign 'G' will be used to designate the set of all taxonomic groups.

(5.2)   The sign 'C' will be used to designate the set of all taxonomic categories.

Taxonomic groups, it will be recalled, are going to be construed as sets of organisms. The set **G** of all taxonomic groups will thus be a set of sets of organisms. The sign 'G', therefore, will belong to name-group N^3. It will appear to the right of 'ϵ' in such statements as '(Primates ϵ G)' and '(Hominidae ϵ G),' which assert that Primates and Homindae are taxonomic groups. Taxonomic categories, on the other hand, are to be construed as sets of taxonomic groups, that is, as sets of sets of organisms. The set **C** of all taxonomic categories will thus be a set of sets of sets of organisms. The sign 'C,' therefore, will belong to name-group N^4. It will appear to the right of 'ϵ' in such statements as '(Genus ϵ C)' and '(Order ϵ C),' which assert that Genus and Order are taxonomic categories.

The sets **G** and **C** are related in the following way: every taxonomic group is a member of some taxonomic category, and every member of some taxonomic category is a taxonomic group. This matter of fact is recorded by the postulate below:

(5.3)   For all x, $(x \in G)$ if and only if there is some y such that $(x \in y)$ and $(y \in C)$.

In the sequel, we shall assume that the set of all organisms is a member of G and also that the set whose sole member is the set of all organisms is a member of C. These assumptions are not usually made in taxonomy, but nothing would seem to prohibit their being made and they will simplify our forthcoming definition of 'taxonomic classificatory system.'

Let us now proceed. The next sign to be introduced—'$IC(u)$'—is a purely logical one. It will designate a relation and will appear in such contexts as '$((x;y) \in IC(u))$,' which may be given the reading 'the set x *immediately contains* the set y, with respect to the set u,' or, more briefly, 'the set x immediately u-contains the set y.' The use of this sign is fixed by the following rule:

(5.4) $((x;y) \in IC(u))$ if and only if $(x \in u)$ and $(y \in u)$, and $(y \subset x)$ and $(y \neq x)$, and there is no z such that $(z \in u)$ and $(z \neq x)$ and $(z \neq y)$ and $(y \subset z)$ and $(z \subset x)$.

If, for instance, we take x as $\{w_1, w_2, w_3\}$ and y as $\{w_1, w_2\}$ and u as $\{x, y\}$, then $(x;y)$ is an $IC(u)$-pair, since both y and x are members of u, and y is included in but not identical with x, and there is no z in u, different from both y and x, in which y is included and which is included in x. But if x is taken as $\{w_1, w_2, w_3\}$ and y is taken as $\{w_1\}$ and u is taken as $\{x, y, \{w_1, w_2\}\}$, then $(x;y)$ is *not* an $IC(u)$-pair, for, although all other conditions are fulfilled, yet there *is* a z in u (namely, $\{w_1, w_2\}$), distinct from both x and y, in which y is included and which is included in x. Turning to **SMP**, and taking u as **S**, it is easy to show that every **SMP**-pair is also an IC(S)-pair. Consider the **SMP**-pair $(G_2;G_8)$, for example. From the definition of 'S' we know that both $(G_2 \, \epsilon \, S)$ and $(G_8 \, \epsilon \, S)$. Furthermore, by (4.22), G_8 is included in G_2; and, by (4.19), G_8 is not identical with G_2. Finally, by (4.23) we know that there is no z in **S**, different from both G_8 and G_0, in which G_8 is included and which is included in G_0. Hence, all requirements being satisfied, $(G_0;G_8)$ is a pair in IC(S). In exactly analogous fashion, each other **SMP**-pair can be shown to be a pair in IC(S). Conversely, it is a fact that each IC(S)-pair is also a pair in **SMP** (the verification of this is left to the reader), and, hence, that:

(5.5)   (SMP = IC(S)).

Thus, **SMP** is identical with the relation of immediate containment with respect to **S**.

Now, this result is most important to our enterprise. For we have just succeeded in showing that at least one taxonomic system in miniature, namely, **SMP**, is identical with the relation of immediate containment when the latter is relativized to a suitable set, in this case **S**. And this suggests that in so far as **SMP** is typical of taxonomic classificatory systems in general, we shall be justified in supposing that any other taxonomic system is a relation that, for some choice of u, is identical with $IC(u)$. Put in these terms, the problem of defining 'taxonomic classificatory system' reduces to the problem of discovering what necessary and sufficient conditions must be imposed upon u in order to make $IC(u)$ a taxonomic system. Let us pursue this suggestion as far as we can. After formulating and rejecting four preliminary definitions we shall arrive at a fifth that will be retained as adequate.

The first definition, using '$(z \, \epsilon \, \textbf{TCS})$' to mean that z is a taxonomic classificatory system, reads as follows:

(i) $(z \, \epsilon \, \textbf{TCS})$ if and only if there is some u such that $(z = IC(u))$.

Of course, this definition is too wide. For 'IC(u)' has been defined in such a way that no restriction whatsoever is put upon the kinds of sets that may belong to u. The relation of immediate u-containment may hold between sets of organisms, machines, houses, numbers, cells—and so on. But if z is to be a taxonomic system, each z-pair has got to be a pair of *taxonomic groups*. Hence, if we are going to try to define '**TCS**' in terms of 'IC(u),' u will obviously have to be a set of taxonomic groups. This restriction can be incorporated into (i) by inserting the clause '($u \subset$ **G**).' This step gives us our second definition:

(ii)   ($z \in$ **TCS**) if and only if there is some u such that ($z =$ IC(u)) and ($u \subset$ **G**).

But this definition is not yet adequate; for it is satisfied by relations that we would hesitate to view as taxonomic systems. It is characteristic not only of **SMP**, but also of other taxonomic systems, that when a taxonomic group (e.g., Primates) is classified into two or more immediately contained subgroups (e.g., Prosimii and Anthropoidea), these subgroups are mutually exclusive, i.e., have no member organisms in common. For **SMP** this was stated by (4.21). But definition (ii) will be satisfied by a system in which some group in its field is split up into several different immediately contained groups, *each one of which overlaps every other*. (The reader may construct an abstract model, if he wishes). In order to rule out such cases, which are not exemplified by actual classificatory systems constructed by taxonomists, we must insert into our definition a still further restriction, whose form is suggested by (4.21). This will give us a third definition:

(iii)   ($z \in$ **TCS**) if and only if there is some u such that ($z =$ IC(u)) and ($u \subset$ **G**) and, for all x, all y, and all w, if (($x;y$) $\in$ IC(u)) and (($x;w$) $\in$ IC(u)) and ($y \neq w$) then (($y \cap w$) = EM).

Thus amended, our definition is still not satisfactory. Among its least important defects is that it allows u to be *redundant*. **SMP** and **S** satisfy it (put '**SMP**' for 'z' and '**S**' for u); but it will also be satisfied by **SMP** in conjunction with many other sets of taxonomic groups in which **S** is included. Consider for example, the set that is obtained by adding to **S** the taxonomic groups (mutually exclusive of each other and of the members of **S**) Insecta, Mollusca, and Planta, i.e., $\{G_0, G_1, \ldots, G_{11},$ Insecta, Mollusca, Planta$\}$. Call this set 'K.' Then, **SMP** will be identical with IC(K), as well as with IC(S), as the reader may prove for himself. Now, the fact that the requirements of (iii) can be met by such queer choices of u (with respect to **SMP**) is not a serious disadvantage but a definition that permits it is inelegant. The way to keep better control over choices of u, however, is pointed out clearly when the relation between **SMP** and **S** is considered, for **S** is the *field* of **SMP**. If we add the clause '$(u \subset \text{FIELD} ' z)$' to (iii), therefore, then choices of u cannot be choices of redundant sets. This yields a fourth definition:

(iv) $(z \in \textbf{TCS})$ if and only if there is some u such that $(u \subset \text{FIELD} ' z)$ and $(z = \text{IC}(u))$ and $(u \subset \textbf{G})$ and, for all x, all y, and all w, if $((x;y) \in \text{IC}(u))$ and $((x;w) \in \text{IC}(u))$ and $(y \neq w)$ then $((y \cap w) = \text{EM})$.

We are now very close to what we are after, but a final defect of (iv) must first be removed.

Let us illustrate this defect by reference to **SMP**. First, let:

$$(\textbf{SMP}' = (\textbf{SMP} \restriction \{G_3, G_9, G_{10}, G_{11}\})),$$

and let:

$$(\textbf{SMP}'' = (\textbf{SMP} \restriction \{G_2, G_6, G_7, G_8\})).$$

Then, let:

$$(\textbf{SMP}''' = (\textbf{SMP}' \cup \textbf{SMP}'')).$$

Thus, **SMP'''** is the set-theoretical sum of two subrelations of **SMP**. It is itself a relation, therefore, and it may be arrow diagramed as follows:

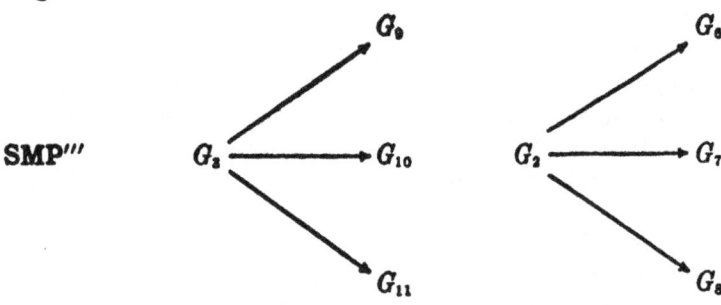

The diagram of **SMP'''** is just that obtained by setting side by side the separate diagrams of **SMP'** and **SMP''**. Now, by referring to (iv), taking z as **SMP'''**, and u as $\{G_3, G_9, G_{10}, G_{11}, G_2, G_6, G_7, G_8\}$, it can easily be shown that **SMP'''** is a taxonomic classificatory system, i.e., that (**SMP'''** ϵ **TCS**). But this is just what we would *not* say, ordinarily. We would say, rather, that **SMP'''** consists of *two* systems (extremely miniature ones), but not that it itself is a classificatory system. What (iv) demands of us is that the set-theoretical sum of any two taxonomic systems whatever be regarded as a taxonomic system—even, for example, were one a classification of plants and the other a classification of animals. But, although we may find in taxonomic literature such titles as "A classification of reptiles" and "A classification of vascular plants," we never find such titles as "A classification of vascular plants and reptiles." What we want from our definition is some formal expression of the fact that a taxonomic system is a structure generated by repeatedly splitting a *single* initial taxonomic group into mutually exclusive subsets that are themselves taxonomic groups; and this can be insured, of course, by inserting the clause '(z ϵ HR)' into (iv). For, by demanding that every member of **TCS** be a hierarchy, we are requiring that it have a unique beginner, and this requirement rules out such cases as **SMP'''**, and others, which have *more* than one beginner. Finally, therefore, we arrive at the following definition of **TCS**:

(5.6)   (**TCS** $=$ the set in which any relation z is a member if and only if $(z \ \epsilon \ \text{HR})$ and there is some u such that $(u \ \subset \ \text{FIELD} \ ' \ z)$ and $(z \ = \ \text{IC}(u))$ and $(u \ \subset \ \textbf{G})$ and, for all x, all y, and all w, if $((x;y) \ \epsilon \ \text{IC}(u))$ and $((x;w) \ \epsilon \ \text{IC}(u))$ and $(y \ne w)$ then $((y \cap w) \ = \ \text{EM}))$.

This definition, it is hoped, will be satisfied by all and only those systems of taxonomic groups that taxonomists are willing to call taxonomic classificatory systems.* Now one way to test a definition is to see what it commits one to, and we may pause now to mention a few of the logical consequences of (5.6).

First of all, we are committed to the view that every taxonomic system is a hierarchy:

(5.7)   For all z, if $(z \ \epsilon \ \textbf{TCS})$ then $(z \ \epsilon \ \text{HR})$,

and this alone presupposes acceptance of a good many other theorems, a very few of which are cited below. (The author is indebted to Professor J. H. Woodger for permission to use some hitherto unpublished theorems dealing with hierarchies.)

---

*Since formulating (5.6) I have discovered a much neater and otherwise more satisfactory definition of 'TCS'. The new definition stipulates that a relation z is to be regarded as a taxonomic classificatory system just in case these four conditions are satisfied: (1) the field of z is included in **G**; (2) there exists a member of the field of z in which every member of the field of z is included; (3) given any members x and y of the field of z, x bears z to y if and only if y is included in but not identical with x and there exists no third member of the field of z in which y is included and which is included in x; and (4) given any members x and y of the field of z, either x bears z to y or else y bears z to x or else the overlap of x and y is identical with the empty set. If the postulate is adopted that the empty set is not a member of **G**, then the right hand side of (5.6) is a logical consequence of these four conditions together with the definitions of '$\text{IC}(u)$' and 'HR'.

Every taxonomic system is a one-many relation:

(5.8)   For all z, if ($z \in$ **TCS**) then ($z \in$ One-Many).

Every taxonomic system has a unique beginner:

(5.9)   For all z, if ($z \in$ **TCS**) then there is an x such that
           ($x = $ B ' z).

If z is any taxonomic system then its converse domain is
identical with the set of all those taxonomic groups that stand
in $\check{z}_{po}$ to the beginner of z:

(5.10)   For all z, if ($z \in$ **TCS**) then ($\check{z}$ " UN $= \check{z}_{po}$ " {B ' z}).

The domain, converse domain, and field of every taxonomic
system is non-empty:

(5.11)   For all z, if ($z \in$ **TCS**) then (z " UN $\neq$ EM) and
           ($\check{z}$ " UN $\neq$ EM) and (FIELD ' $z \neq$ EM).

If z is a **TCS** then the first constituent of each z-pair is distinct
from its second constituent:

(5.12)   For all z, if ($z \in$ **TCS**) then, for all x and all y, if
           (($x;y$) $\in z$) then ($x \neq y$).

This is the general statement of what was asserted, in (4.19),
of **SMP** in particular. Even more generally:

(5.13)   For all z, if ($z \in$ **TCS**) then, for all x and all y, if
           (($x;y$) $\in z_{po}$) then ($x \neq y$).

If z is a **TCS**, then everything (taxonomic group) to which the
beginner stands in z_{po} has something standing in z to it, and
vice versa:

(5.14)   For all z, if ($z \in$ **TCS**) then, for all x, ((B ' $z;x$) $\in z_{po}$)
           if and only if there is some y such that (($y;x$) $\in z$).

If x and y are distinct levels of the same taxonomic system, then they have no members in common:

(5.15)   For all z, if $(z \in \textbf{TCS})$ then, for all x and all y, if $(x \in \text{LEV} \text{ `` } \{z\})$ and $(y \in \text{LEV} \text{ `` } \{z\})$ and $(x \neq y)$ then $((x \cap y) = \text{EM})$.

(This utilizes 0.93 of Woodger's *The Axiomatic Method in Biology*.)

The reverse of any z-pair in a taxonomic system z is not itself a member of the system:

(5.16)   For all z, if $(z \in \textbf{TCS})$ then, for all x and all y, if $((x;y) \in z)$ then it is *not* the case that $((y;x) \in z)$.

That is to say, every taxonomic system is an *asymmetrical* relation.

No member of the field of a taxonomic system z bears z to itself:

(5.17)   For all z, if $(z \in \textbf{TCS})$ then, for all x, if $(x \in \text{FIELD} \text{ ` } z)$ then it is not the case that $((x;x) \in z)$.

That is, every taxonomic system is an *irreflexive* relation.

If $(x;y)$ and $(y;w)$ are both pairs in a taxonomic system z, then $(x;w)$ is not a pair in z:

(5.18)   For all z, if $(z \in \textbf{TCS})$ then, for all x, all y, and all w, if $((x;y) \in z)$ and $((y;w) \in z)$ then it is *not* the case that $((x;w) \in z)$.

Thus, every taxonomic system is an *intransitive* relation.

(Hitherto, we have not employed such expressions as 'z is asymmetrical,' 'z is irreflexive,' and 'z is intransitive'; but they are *defined*, respectively, by the expressions following 'For all z, if $(z \in \textbf{TCS})$ then' in (5.16), (5.17), and (5.18).)

These theorems have all followed from the occurrence of

'($z \epsilon$ HR)' in the definition of 'TCS.' Let us now present a few theorems depending upon other clauses in the definition.

Every member of the field of a taxonomic system is a taxonomic group:

(5.19)   For all z, if ($z \epsilon$ TCS) then, for all x, if ($x \epsilon$ FIELD ' z) then ($x \epsilon$ G).

Each member of the field of a taxonomic system belongs to some taxonomic category:

(5.20)   For all z, if ($z \epsilon$ TCS) then, for all x, if ($x \epsilon$ FIELD ' z) then there is some y such that ($x \epsilon y$) and ($y \epsilon$ C).

Every taxonomic system is identical with IC(u), for some choice of u:

(5.21)   For all z, if ($z \epsilon$ TCS) then there is some u such that ($z = $ IC(u)).

Every member of the field of a taxonomic system is included in the beginner of the system:

(5.22)   For all z, if ($z \epsilon$ TCS) then, for all x, if ($x \epsilon$ FIELD ' z) then ($x \subset$ B ' z).

If z is a taxonomic system then the second constituent of each z-pair is included in the first constituent of that pair:

(5.23)   For all z, if ($z \epsilon$ TCS) then, for all x and all y, if ((x;y) ϵz) then ($y \subset x$).

This theorem generalizes (4.22). Even more generally:

(5.24)   For all z, if ($z \epsilon$ TCS) then, for all x and all y, if ((x;y) ϵ *z) then ($y \subset x$).

If z is a taxonomic system and x and y are any two members of its field then y is included in x, or x is included in y, or x and y are mutually exclusive:

(5.25)   For all z, if ($z \in$ **TCS**) then, for all x and all y, if
          ($x \in$ FIELD ' z) and ($y \in$ FIELD ' z) then ($y \subset x$)
          or ($x \subset y$) or (($x \cap y$) = EM).

Finally, we have as a consequence of the foregoing that the
converse of a taxonomic system is never a taxonomic system:

(5.26)   For all z, if ($z \in$ **TCS**) then it is not the case that
          ($\breve{z} \in$ **TCS**).

Now, the foregoing are by no means exhaustive of the theorems
that are obtainable as consequences of the definition of 'TCS';
but they will serve, perhaps, to indicate some of the statements
about taxonomic systems that must be accepted if the definition
is accepted. There is no obvious reason to expect that taxonomists will reject them.

It is worth pointing out that not *every* statement about taxonomic systems will follow from the definition of 'TCS.' Were
we developing an axiomatized theory of taxonomic systems, a
good many statements would have to be adopted as postulates.
For example, it will not follow from our definition that every
taxonomic system is a *finite* hierarchy. (Roughly speaking, an
infinite hierarchy is one whose converse has no beginner; cf.
Woodger, 1937, page 43.) To insure this we should have to lay
down some postulate such as that for every taxonomic system
there is some level of it that is included in the beginners of the
converse of the system:

    For all z, if ($z \in$ **TCS**) then there is some x such that
    ($x \in$ LEV " $\{z\}$) and ($x \subset$ B " $\{\breve{z}\}$).

Or we should have to derive it from some assumptions not here
stated. Perhaps even the assumption that there are a finite
number of taxonomic groups would do the trick.

6. *Taxonomic Systems and Taxonomic Categories*

Thus far, strangely enough, we have had to say practically nothing about the relations between taxonomic systems and their associated categories. We do have a theorem (5.20) guaranteeing membership, in some category, of each taxonomic group in the field of a taxonomic system; but we have no account yet of the relations of taxonomic categories to each other and to various structural parts of taxonomic systems. In this section we shall consider a few of the many problems connected with these topics.

Let us now recall the categories associated with **SMP**. These may be obtained by referring to the extract from Simpson's classification of mammals (4.4), or by glancing back at the diagram of **SMP** (4.9). From either of these sources, it should be easy to see that the following statements hold:

(6.1) $(G_0 \; \epsilon \; \text{Order})$,

$(G_1 \; \epsilon \; \text{Suborder})$,

$(G_2 \; \epsilon \; \text{Suborder})$,

$(G_3 \; \epsilon \; \text{Infraorder})$,

$(G_4 \; \epsilon \; \text{Infraorder})$,

$(G_5 \; \epsilon \; \text{Infraorder})$,

$(G_6 \; \epsilon \; \text{Superfamily})$,

$(G_7 \; \epsilon \; \text{Superfamily})$,

$(G_8 \; \epsilon \; \text{Superfamily})$,

(G_9 ∈ Superfamily),
(G_{10} ∈ Superfamily),
(G_{11} ∈ Superfamily).

Furthermore, obviously, we have:

(6.2)   (Order ∈ **C**),
(Suborder ∈ **C**),
(Infraorder ∈ **C**),
(Superfamily ∈ **C**).

We shall say that x is a category *associated with* a taxonomic system z, or that x is z-associated, or, symbolically, that $((x;z)$ ∈ **CA**), just in case some member of the field of z is a member of x:

(6.3) $((x;z)$ ∈ **CA**) if and only if $(x$ ∈ **C**) and $(z$ ∈ **TCS**) and there is some y such that $(y$ ∈ $x)$ and $(y$ ∈ FIELD ' $z)$.

For example, since each of Order, Suborder, Infraorder, and Superfamily are members of **C**, since (**SMP** ∈ **TCS**), and since each of G_0, G_2, . . . , G_{11} is a member of FIELD ' **SMP**, it is plain that each of the following is a true statement:

(6.4)   ((Order; **SMP**) ∈ **CA**),
((Suborder; **SMP**) ∈ **CA**),
((Infraorder; **SMP**) ∈ **CA**),
((Superfamily; **SMP**) ∈ **CA**).

That is to say, each of the four categories mentioned in these statements is **SMP**-associated. Furthermore, it should be apparent that if z is any taxonomic system then **CA** " $\{z\}$ is the set of all z-associated categories. For example:

(6.5)   (**CA** " $\{$**SMP**$\}$ = $\{$Order, Suborder, Infraorder, Superfamily$\}$).

To see how the categories associated with a taxonomic system are related among themselves will require, along with other things, the introduction of a new logical sign 'M' designating the relation between member and set. We shall say that $(x;y)$ is a pair in M just in case x is a member of y:

(6.6)   (M = the relation in which any pair $(x;y)$ is a member
          if and only if $(x \in y)$).

Using this notation, the twelve statements of (6.1) can be rewritten as follows:

(6.7) $((G_0; \text{Order}) \in M)$,

          $((G_1; \text{Suborder}) \in M)$,

          $((G_2; \text{Suborder}) \in M)$,

          $((G_3; \text{Infraorder}) \in M)$,

          . . . .

          $((G_8; \text{Superfamily}) \in M)$,

          $((G_9; \text{Superfamily}) \in M)$,

          . . . .

Were such statements *all* that we could formulate with the help of 'M,' we could abandon the latter altogether in favor of the familiar epsilon notation. But we can use 'M' to construct statements that cannot be written in terms of 'ϵ.' For, if M is the relation of member to set, then, clearly, M̌ is the relation of set to member. Hence, for example, we have:

(6.8) $((\text{Order}; G_0) \in \check{M})$,

          $((\text{Suborder}; G_1) \in \check{M})$,

          $((\text{Suborder}; G_2) \in \check{M})$,

          $((\text{Infraorder}; G_3) \in \check{M})$,

          . . . .

          $((\text{Superfamily}; G_8) \in \check{M})$,

          $((\text{Superfamily}; G_9) \in \check{M})$,

          . . . .

as statements for which there are no counterparts in the epsilon notation. Now, let us put 'M' to work.

Let us use the symbol '**PR**(z)' to mean the relation in which a taxonomic category x stands to a taxonomic category y when x *precedes* y, relative to a taxonomic system z, or briefly, when x z-precedes y. This relation is defined as follows:

(6.9)   (**PR**(z) = the relation in which any pair ($x;y$) is a member if and only if ($x \in$ **CA** " $\{z\}$) and ($y \in$ **CA** " $\{z\}$) and (($x;y) \in (\check{M} \mid z_{p0} \mid M)$)).

From this definition it will follow that x z-precedes y just when x and y are both z-associated categories, and there are taxonomic groups w and u in the field of z which are such that (($x;w) \in \check{M}$) and (($w;u) \in z_{p0}$) and (($u;y) \in M$); i.e., when there is a z_{p0}-pair whose first constituent group is a member of the category x and whose second constituent group is a member of the category y. Perhaps this whole business can be made clearer with the aid of an arrow diagram (6.10).

PR(z)

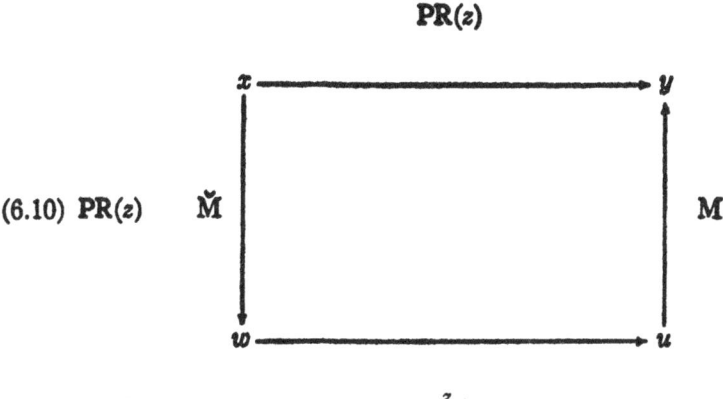

(6.10) **PR(z)** $\check{M}$ M

z_{p0}

In this diagram 'x' and 'y' represent z-associated taxonomic categories; and 'w' and 'u' represent two taxonomic groups in the field of z, of which the first stands in z_{p0} to the second. Each arrow in the diagram is labeled to indicate the relation in which the pair represented with the help of the arrow is a member. Now, what the diagram clearly shows is this: it shows that to say "the designation of y can be reached by going one $\mathbf{PR}(z)$-arrow-step from that of x" is equivalent to saying "the designation of y can be reached from that of x by going one M-converse-arrow-step to the designation of some group w, and then going one z_{p0}-arrow-step to the designation of some group u, and then going one M-arrow-step to the designation of y." Briefly, if x z-precedes y, then some member of x stands in z_{p0} to some member of y.

By compiling a list of $\mathbf{SMP}_{p0}$ pairs (or by consulting the diagram of $\mathbf{SMP}$) and referring to (6.5), (6.7) and (6.8), we can easily establish the following exhaustive list of $\mathbf{PR(SMP)}$-pairs:

(6.11)   ((Order; Suborder) ϵ $\mathbf{PR(SMP)}$),

((Order; Infraorder) ϵ $\mathbf{PR(SMP)}$),

((Order; Superfamily) ϵ $\mathbf{PR(SMP)}$),

((Suborder; Infraorder) ϵ $\mathbf{PR(SMP)}$),

((Suborder; Superfamily) ϵ $\mathbf{PR(SMP)}$),

((Infraorder; Superfamily) ϵ $\mathbf{PR(SMP)}$).

Consider the pair (Order; Superfamily), for example. This is shown to be a $\mathbf{PR(SMP)}$-pair as follows: (1) from (6.5) we see that both Order and Superfamily are members of $\mathbf{CA}$ " $\{\mathbf{SMP}\}$; (2) from (6.8) we find that (Order; G_0) is an $\check{\mathrm{M}}$-pair; (3) from the diagram of $\mathbf{SMP}$ (4.9) it is easy to see that $((G_0; G_8) \epsilon \mathbf{SMP}_{p0})$; and (4) from (6.7) it is apparent that $(G_8;$ Superfamily) is an M-pair. Hence, from (2), (3), and (4)—with the help of (2.20)—it follows that (5) ((Order; Superfamily) ϵ ($\check{\mathrm{M}}$ | $\mathbf{SMP}_{p0}$ | M)). Finally, from (1) and (5) together with (6.9), it follows that ((Order; Superfamily) ϵ $\mathbf{PR(SMP)}$).

Before defining another precedence relation, let us have a

look at some of the properties of z-precedence. It seems to be a matter of fact, although it does not clearly follow from what has already been said, that if a category x stands in z-precedence to a category y then x and y are not identical. This may be confirmed by examining **SMP** and other taxonomic systems. Let us adopt it as a postulate, therefore:

(6.12)   For all x, all y, and all z, if $((x;y) \ \epsilon \ \mathbf{PR}(z))$ then $(x \neq y)$.

Now we may proceed with two theorems and a postulate about z-precedence.

No taxonomic category paired with itself is a $\mathbf{PR}(z)$-pair:

(6.13)   For all x and all z, it is not the case that $((x;x) \ \epsilon \ \mathbf{PR}(z))$.

That is to say, $\mathbf{PR}(z)$ is a totally irreflexive relation.

If $(x;y)$ is a $\mathbf{PR}(z)$-pair then its reverse $(y;x)$ is not:

(6.14)   For all x, all y, and all z, if $((x;y) \ \epsilon \ \mathbf{PR}(z))$ then it is *not* the case that $((y;x) \ \epsilon \ \mathbf{PR}(z))$.

That is, $\mathbf{PR}(z)$ is an asymmetrical relation. We now postulate that if a category is $\mathbf{PR}(z)$-paired with a second and the second is $\mathbf{PR}(z)$-paired with a third, then the first is $\mathbf{PR}(z)$-paired with the third:

(6.15)   For all x, all y, all z, and all w, if $((x;y) \ \epsilon \ \mathbf{PR}(z))$ and $((y;z) \ \epsilon \ \mathbf{PR}(z))$ then $((x;z) \ \epsilon \ \mathbf{PR}(z))$.

Thus, according to (6.15), z-precedence is transitive.

Next, let us define a relation of *immediate z-precedence* using '$\mathbf{IPR}(z)$' to mean the relation of a taxonomic category x to a taxonomic category y when x *immediately* precedes y with respect to the taxonomic system z:

(6.16)   ($\mathbf{IPR}(z)$ = the relation in which any ordered pair $(x;y)$ is a member if and only if $((x;y) \ \epsilon \ \mathbf{PR}(z))$ and there is no w such that $((x;w) \ \epsilon \ \mathbf{PR}(z))$ and $((w;y) \ \epsilon \ \mathbf{PR}(z))$).

That is to say, if x *immediately* z-precedes y then x z-precedes y and there is no intervening third category associated with z. Looking back at the list (6.11) of **PR(SMP)**-pairs, for example, it is quite readily seen that the following are all true statements:

(6.17)   ((Order; Suborder) ϵ **IPR(SMP)**),

((Suborder; Infraorder) ϵ **IPR(SMP)**),

((Infraorder; Superfamily) ϵ **IPR(SMP)**),

and that no other pairs whose constituents are chosen from **CA** " {**SMP**} will be **IPR(SMP)**-pairs. Thus, we have established a unique order among the categories associated with **SMP**.

This result suggests that given any taxonomic system z, a list of M̌-pairs, a list of M-pairs and a list of z_{po}-pairs, we can establish an ordering of the members of **CA** " {z} by using the definition of '**IPR**(z)'. This is not strictly true, however, as we shall point out after presenting a brief list of theorems relating to immediate z-precedence.

No category that is immediately z-precedent to another is identical with it:

(6.18)   For all x, all y, and all z, if $((x;y)$ ϵ **IPR**(z)) then $(x \neq y)$.

Hence, no category is immediately z-precedent to itself:

(6.19)   For all z and all z, it is *not* the case that $((x;x)$ ϵ **IPR**(z)).

If any category-pair is an **IPR**(z)-pair, then its reverse is not:

(6.20)   For all x, all y, and all z, if $((x;y)$ ϵ **IPR**(z)) then it is *not* the case that $((y;x)$ ϵ **IPR**(z)).

Therefore, immediate z-precedence, like z-precedence, is a totally irreflexive and asymmetrical relation. But, unlike z-precedence, immediate z-precedence is an intransitive relation:

(6.21)   For all x, all y, all z, and all w, if $((x;y) \in \mathbf{IPR}(z))$ and $((y;w) \in \mathbf{IPR}(z))$ then it is *not* the case that $((x;w) \in \mathbf{IPR}(z))$

Finally, if x immediately z-precedes y then x stands in $(\check{M} \mid z \mid M)$ to y:

(6.22)   For all x, all y, and all z, $((x;y) \in \mathbf{IPR}(z))$ then $((x;y) \in (\check{M} \mid z \mid M))$.

It is possible to discover systems satisfying the definition of 'TCS' whose associated categories cannot be ordered in the way we have described. Consider, for example, the system $(\mathbf{SMP} \restriction \{G_0, G_1, G_2, G_3, G_6\})$. Call this system '**SMP''''**.' **SMP''''** is included in **SMP**, and its diagram (6.23) will exhibit just four **SMP**-pairs.

(6.23) **SMP''''**

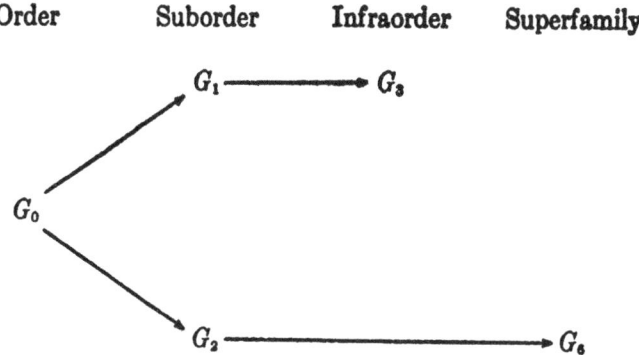

Order	Suborder	Infraorder	Superfamily

From this diagram it is clear that the following **PR** (**SMP''''**)-pairs can be found: (Order; Suborder), (Order; Infraorder), (Order; Superfamily), (Suborder; Infraorder), (Suborder; Superfamily). However, it is not possible to show that (Infraorder; Superfamily) is such a pair, for the simple reason that Infraorder does not bear ($\check{\text{M}}$ | $\textbf{SMP}''''_{\text{p0}}$ | M) to Superfamily, since there is no group w and no group u such that Infraorder bears $\check{\text{M}}$ to w and w bears $\textbf{SMP}''''_{\text{p0}}$ to u and u bears M to Superfamily. But, if it cannot even be shown that Infraorder $\textbf{SMP}''''$-precedes Superfamily, then it cannot be shown that Infraorder *immediately* $\textbf{SMP}''''$-precedes Superfamily. Hence, for this case, our method fails. But this is not a serious drawback, for it is not likely that such artificial examples as $\textbf{SMP}''''$ will be encountered except as subsystems of larger ones (such as $\textbf{SMP}$) in which the group connections that are requisite to establishing precedence relations are apt to occur (as they do in $\textbf{SMP}$). Nevertheless, such examples indicate that (6.9) needs reformulating.

With some exceptions, therefore, it appears that the categories associated with a given taxonomic system z are all related by precedence relations. Each such category, moreover, is related to z by $\textbf{CA}$ and to some member of the field of z by $\check{\text{M}}$, the converse of the membership relation. In the remainder of this section still further relations between the structural elements and the associated categories of taxonomic systems will be considered.

Let us begin with a simple theorem. From what has already been said—especially (6.9) and (6.12)—it follows that if z is a member of $\textbf{TCS}$ then the z-associated categories to which the constituents of z_{p0}-pairs separately belong are nonidentical:

(6.24)   For all z, all x, all y, all w, and all u, if ($z \, \epsilon \, \textbf{TCS}$) and $((x;y) \, \epsilon \, z_{\text{p0}})$ and ($w \, \textbf{CA} \, `` \, \{z\}$) and ($u \, \epsilon \, \textbf{CA} \, `` \, \{z\}$) and ($x \, \epsilon \, w$) and ($y \, \epsilon \, u$) then ($w \neq u$).

With this theorem to help, it is very easy to obtain the following list of inequalities among the categories associated with $\textbf{SMP}$: (Order $\neq$ Suborder), (Order $\neq$ Infraorder), (Order $\neq$ Superfamily), (Suborder $\neq$ Infraorder), (Suborder $\neq$ Superfamily), and (Infraorder $\neq$ Superfamily). This list will be referred to again.

The next item is not clearly forthcoming as a theorem, but it seems to be a true statement about taxonomic systems and their associated categories, nevertheless. Whenever z is a taxonomic system then all second constituents of z-pairs with the same first constituent are members of the same z-associated category. For example, G_1 and G_2 (both are second constituents of **SMP**-pairs whose first constituent is G_0) are both members of Suborder. Similarly G_3, G_4, and G_5 are all members of Infraorder; and G_9, G_{10}, G_{11}, as well as G_6, G_7, G_8, are all members of Superfamily. It seems quite reasonable to adopt the following postulate, therefore:

(6.25)   For all x and all z, if ($z \,\epsilon\,$ **TCS**) and ($x \,\epsilon\,$ FIELD ' z) and ($\breve{z}$ " $\{x\}$ $\neq$ EM) then there is a y such that ($y \,\epsilon\,$ CA " $\{z\}$) and ($\breve{z}$ " $\{x\}$ $\subset y$).

In familiar language, this postulate says that if any taxonomic group in the field of a taxonomic system is split up into several immediately contained subgroups then the latter are all members of the same taxonomic category. No exceptions to this rule are known to the author.

Relations between the *levels* of a taxonomic system and the categories associated with that system are less easy to generalize about. Consider **SMP**, whose levels are listed in (4.18). The *zero*-th level of **SMP** is included in Order, for its sole member is G_0 and ($G_0 \,\epsilon\,$ Order). The *first* level of **SMP** is included in Suborder, for its sole members are G_1 and G_2 and both of these are members of Suborder. Similarly, the *third* level of **SMP** is included in Superfamily, for its sole members are G_9, G_{10}, and G_{11}—each of which is a member of Superfamily. The *second* level of **SMP**, however, is included in no taxonomic category whatsoever. For this level—i.e., $\{G_3,G_4,G_5,G_6,G_7,G_8\}$—has some members ($G_3,G_4,G_5$) that belong to Infraorder, and some (G_6,G_7,G_8)

that belong to Superfamily; and, as we have already seen in connection with (6.24), (Infraorder $\neq$ Superfamily). In general, if any taxonomic system has a level any two of whose members belong to different categories associated with the system, then that level is included in no category associated with the system. If the reader will examine various taxonomic systems and make arrow diagrams of them, he will see that in a great many systems there will be one or more levels of this kind. Hence, were we axiomatizing taxonomic theory, we should require the following statement either as a postulate or as a theorem:

(6.26)   For some x and some z, $(z \, \epsilon \, \text{TCS})$ and $(x \, \epsilon \, \text{LEV}$ " $\{z\})$ and there is no y such that $(x \subset y)$ and $(y \, \epsilon \, \text{CA}$ " $\{z\})$.

That is to say, there are taxonomic systems with levels that are not included in any category associated with the system. On the other hand, we shall have to admit that *every* taxonomic system has *at least two* levels each of which is included in some category associated with the system:

(6.27)   For all z, if $(z \, \epsilon \, \text{TCS})$ then, for some x, some y, some w, and some u, $(x \, \epsilon \, \text{LEV}$ " $\{z\})$ and $(y \, \epsilon \, \text{LEV}$ " $\{z\})$ and $(x \neq y)$ and $(x \subset w)$ and $(y \subset u)$ and $(w \, \epsilon \, \text{CA}$ " $\{z\})$ and $(u \, \epsilon \, \text{CA}$ " $\{z\})$.

And this statement is not a postulate, it is a logical *consequence* of the definition of 'TCS,' in conjunction with the definition of 'CA' and postulate (6.25). This is not hard to see. For, by the definition of 'TCS' every taxonomic system has in its field exactly one taxonomic group (in some category) that is its unique beginner. Hence, the set whose sole member is this group is the *zero*-th level of the system. Since this beginner belongs to some category, that category (by the definition of 'CA') is associated with the system. Hence, the *zero*-th level is included in a category associated with the system. Furthermore, similarly, it will follow with the help of postulate (6.25) that the *first* level of every taxonomic system is included in some category associated with the system. Thus, the *zero*-th and first levels of any **TCS** each will be included in some category associated with it:

(6.28)   For all z, if $(z \ \epsilon \ \textbf{TCS})$ then there is some x and some y such that $(x \ \epsilon \ \text{CA} \ `` \ \{z\})$ and $(y \ \epsilon \ \textbf{CA} \ `` \ \{z\})$ and $(\text{LEV}_0 \ ` \ z \subset x)$ and $(\text{LEV}_1 \ ` \ z \subset y)$.

About succeeding levels, no such generalization can be made.

The problems involved in explicating the relationships between structural parts of taxonomic systems and categories associated with the latter are enormously complicated by still further difficulties, one of which will now be considered. When a taxonomist is handed a specimen x and asked to detail its taxonomic affiliations, he will generally do so in the following way. He will choose some taxonomic system z, and make a list of all those taxonomic groups in the field of z in which x is a member. To such a list he will append a list of z-associated taxonomic categories, one for each listed taxonomic group. The result will be a citation of the sort illustrated by (4.3), for example, and we may consider still another taken from the same source as that one:

(6.29)   Class : Mammalia
             Subclass : Theria
                Infraclass : Eutheria
                   Cohort : Mutica
                      Order : Cetacea
                         Suborder : Mysticeti
                            Family : Rhachianectidae
                               Genus : *Rhachianectes*

Still others will be found in every biology textbook. In such a citation no category is named more than once, and each category name appears in apposition to exactly one group name. It is not unfair, therefore, to suppose that their authors believe that no taxonomic group is named more than once in such a list; and from this it follows that they must subscribe also to the following postulate:

> No taxonomic group in the field of a given system is a member of more than one category associated with that system;

or, more precisely:

(i)   For all z, all y, and all w, if $(z \in \mathbf{TCS})$ and $(y \in \mathbf{CA}\,"\{z\})$ and $(w \in \mathbf{CA}\,"\,\{z\})$ and $(((y \cap w) \cap \text{FIELD}\,`z) \neq \text{EM})$, then $(y = w)$.

A logical consequence of (i) is:

(ii)   For all z, all y, and all w, if $(z \in \mathbf{TCS})$ and $(y \in \mathbf{CA}\,"\{z\})$ and $(w \in \mathbf{CA}\,"\{z\})$ and $(y \neq w)$, then $(((y \cap w) \cap \text{FIELD}\,`z) = \text{EM})$.

That is to say, no two z-associated categories overlap; or, as it would ordinarily be phrased, no species is a genus, no genus is a family, no family is a subclass, and so on.

Now, it frequently happens that a taxonomic group in one taxonomic category will have a single subgroup in another category. Many such cases are familiar to students of taxonomy, but for illustration one or two examples will suffice. In Bentham and Hooker's system, for instance (see Bentham, 1892), the genus *Montia* includes the single species *Montia fontana* (water chickweed), and the genus *Conium* includes the single species *Conium maculatum* (hemlock). (It should be noted that when Bentham and Hooker say that a genus has a single species contained in it, they do not limit themselves to species whose members occur only in Britain.) Similarly, in Simpson's classification of mammals, we find that the cohort Mutica contains a single order, Cetacea, and that the family Rhachianectidae contains a single genus *Rhachianectes* (gray whales). Let us now see what are some of the logical consequences of such facts. We may as well continue to draw upon Simpson's classificatory system for illustrative material.

First let us adopt a name for Simpson's entire classificatory system: let us call it 'SCM.' Let us assume, furthermore, that it is a member of TCS. Then clearly, we shall have both of the following statements:

(6.30)   (Cohort ϵ **CA** " {**SCM**}),

(6.31)   (Order ϵ **CA** " {**SCM**}),

and also (see (6.29)):

(6.32)   (Mutica ϵ Cohort) and (Mutica ϵ FIELD 'z)),

(6.33)   ((Cetacea ϵ Order and (Cetacea ϵ FIELD 'z)).

Furthermore, by consulting Simpson's monograph, it is easy to verify that:

(6.34)   (Cohort $\neq$ Order).

From the indentations employed in presenting **SCM** it is clear that every organism that belongs to Cetacea will also belong to Mutica. That is:

(6.35)   (Cetacea $\subset$ Mutica).

What the indentations fail to suggest is that every organism belonging to Mutica also belongs to Cetacea, although it is clearly the author's intent to classify all muticans as cetaceans. Hence, we have:

(6.36)   (Mutica $\subset$ Cetacea).

But, from (6.35) and (6.36) it follows, by (1.2), that Mutica and Cetacea are identical taxonomic groups:

(6.37)   (Mutica = Cetacea).

In other words, the group names 'Mutica' and 'Cetacea' both name the same group of mammalian organisms. Next, by utilizing a hitherto unmentioned set-theoretical law which reads 'if $(x = y)$ and $(y \, \epsilon \, z)$ then $(x \, \epsilon \, z)$,' we may infer from (6.37), (6.32), and (6.33) that Cetacea is a cohort and that Mutica is an order:

(6.38)   (Cetacea ϵ Cohort).

(6.39)   (Mutica ϵ Order).

Furthermore, by using (1.13), we may infer from (6.33) and (6.38) that Cetacea is both a cohort and an order in the field of z:

(6.40)   (Cetacea ϵ ((Cohort $\cap$ Order) $\cap$ FIELD 'z)).

Similarly, we have, from (6.32) and (6.39), that Mutica, also, is both a cohort and an order in the field of z:

(6.41)   (Mutica ϵ ((Cohort $\cap$ Order) $\cap$ FIELD 'z)).

Now, these two last results will sound most strangely in taxonomic ears, and there may even be some taxonomists who will deny that they are true, but it is not clearly evident (to say the least) that they can be escaped. In any case, from either (6.40) or (6.41) we may infer:

(6.42)   (((Cohort $\cap$ Order) $\cap$ FIELD 'z) $\neq$ EM).

Thus, we have shown that Cohort and Order are overlapping categories. Hence, collecting (6.30), (6.31), (6.34), and (6.42), we have, with the help of the assumption that (**SCM** ϵ **TCS**):

(6.43)   (**SCM** ϵ **TCS**) and (Cohort ϵ **CA** "{**SCM**}) and (Order ϵ **CA** "{**SCM**}) and (Cohort $\neq$ Order) and (((Cohort $\cap$ Order) $\cap$ FIELD '**SCM**) $\neq$ EM).

Finally, from (6.43) we may infer:

(6.44) There is a z, a y, and a w such that $(z \; \epsilon \; \textbf{TCS})$ and $(y \; \epsilon \; \textbf{CA} \; "\{z\})$ and $(w \; \epsilon \; \textbf{CA} \; "\{z\})$ and $(y \neq w)$ and $(((y \cap w) \cap \text{FIELD} \; 'z) \neq \text{EM})$.

But this, it so happens, is the logical contradictory of postulate (ii), which must, therefore, be abandoned if (6.44) is true. But if (ii) is rejected then (i) must be also—for (i) is true only if (ii) is.

The point brought out by this example is that the taxonomic categories associated with a given system are not always mutually exclusive sets of taxonomic groups. In most taxonomic systems the categories overlap in various ways. We have seen one example from Simpson's classification; and by similar reasoning we can also show that in his system ((Family $\cap$ Genus) $\neq$ EM), for the family Rhachianectidae and its only genus *Rhachianectes* are one and the same set of organisms. But all of this tends to be hidden by indentational conventions, and also, probably, by the failure of taxonomists to provide themselves with adequate criteria of group identity. A less misleading—but unorthodox—version of (6.29) might be written as follows:

(6.45) Class : Mammalia
    Subclass : Theria
        Infraclass : Eutheria
            (Cohort $\cap$ Order) : Mutica, Cetacea
            Suborder : Mysticeti
                (Family $\cap$ Genus) : Rhachianectidae,
                              Rhachianectes.

A good example of the overlapping of three different categories is exhibited in bird taxonomy. According to Peters (1931), all birds in the order Apterygiformes are classified in a single family Apterygidae and a single genus *Apteryx*. Hence, relative to this system, we have a set of organisms that is simultaneously an order, a family, and a genus; i.e., ((Order ∩ (Family ∩ Genus)) ≠ EM).

It is not hard to see how category overlapping hopelessly complicates the problem of stating anything general about the relations between the levels of a taxonomic system and the categories associated with that system—for not only may a single category have its membership distributed over several levels (cf. **SMP**), but also a single level may have its membership distributed over several categories (cf. (6.45)). For these reasons, and not only these, the whole theory of categorical association needs to be much further clarified.

Selected Bibliography

Bentham, George. 1892. Handbook of the British flora. Sixth edition, revised by J. D. Hooker. L. Reeve & Co., London.

Hilbert, D., and W. Ackermann. 1950. Principles of mathematical logic. Chelsea, New York. A standard textbook of modern logic.

Langer, S. K. 1937. An introduction to symbolic logic. Houghton Mifflin Co., New York. Contains a detailed introduction to elementary set-theory.

Lawrence, G. H. M. 1951. Taxonomy of vascular plants. Macmillan, New York. Covers practically the entire range of botanical systematics. Highly recommended.

Mayr, E., E. G. Linsley, and R. Usinger. 1953. Methods and principles of systematic zoology. McGraw-Hill Book Co., New York. A general treatment of classificatory procedures in zoological taxonomy.

Peters, J. L. 1931. Check list of birds of the world. Vol. 1. Harvard University Press, Cambridge, Mass.

Quine, W. V. 1950. Methods of logic. Henry Holt and Co., New York. One of the very best introductions to logical methods and theory. Highly recommended.

—— 1951. Mathematical logic. Revised edition. Harvard University Press, Cambridge, Mass. An advanced treatment of modern formal logic. Notable for rigor and clarity of exposition.

Simpson, G. G. 1945. The principles of classification and a classification of mammals. Bulletin of the American Museum of Natural History, Vol. 85, 350 pp.

Whitehead, A. N., and B. Russell. 1910–1913. Principia mathematica. 3 vols. Second edition, 1925–1927. Cambridge University Press, Cambridge, England. This great work is the classic English treatise on modern mathematical logic.

Woodger, J. H. 1937. The axiomatic method in biology. Cambridge University Press, Cambridge, England. The first serious attempt to formalize certain branches of biological theory. Contains practically all of the author's work on the abstract theory of hierarchies. An excellent introduction to *Principia mathematica*.

—— 1951. Science without properties, The British Journal for the Philosophy of Science, 2: 193–216.

—— 1952. From biology to mathematics, The British Journal for the Philosophy of Science, 3: 1–21. On p. 11 will be found the definition of "hieıarchy" that has been used in the present essay. This article, together with the immediately preceding one, should interest those taxonomists who wish to regard taxonomic groups as spatiotemporal objects rather than as abstract sets. The author develops a simple language, with a structure entirely different from that of set theory, in which taxonomic group names may be construed as names of individuals—see expecially pages 19-21 of the 1952 article.

Acknowledgments

The Author acknowledges with gratitude the generosity shown by the following in making the publication of the Bicentennial Editions and Studies possible: the Trustees of Columbia University, the Trustees of Columbia University Press, Mrs. W. Murray Crane, Mr. James Grossman, Mr. Herman Wouk, and friends of the late Robert Pitney who wish to remain anonymous.

Bei Fragen zur Produktsicherheit wenden Sie sich bitte an:
If you have any questions regarding product safety,
please contact:

Walter de Gruyter GmbH
Genthiner Straße 13
10785 Berlin
productsafety@degruyterbrill.com